Leaving Faith Behind

Leaving Faith Behind

The journeys and
perspectives of people
who have chosen to
leave Islam

EDITED BY

Fiyaz Mughal
and Aliyah
Saleem

DARTON · LONGMAN + TODD

First published in 2018 by
Darton, Longman and Todd Ltd
1 Spencer Court
140 – 142 Wandsworth High Street
London SW18 4JJ

ISBN: 978-0-232-53364-4

A catalogue record for this book is available from the British Library

Printed and bound in Great Britain by Bell & Bain, Glasgow

CONTENTS

PREFACE

Apostasy – the act of disaffiliation from one's faith – is an issue which is misunderstood, and it affects millions of people today. The rejection of believing in a deity, of the belief in some supernatural power, is a fundamental human right; however, unfortunately, this right is not afforded to everyone. What should be a personal decision for the individual is shrouded in fear of 'coming out', because the environment around leaving Islam has become so highly charged. Layered onto this is a fear of losing family connections, friends, social status and ultimately of becoming a pariah and outcast. For migrants who came to the UK in the last sixty years, one of their ties to each other was their faith, which was also bound tightly with a culture heavily influenced by Islam.

Allied to these fears, for those thinking of leaving Islam there is a fear of the 'afterlife'. Like Christianity, Islam is focused on undertaking deeds in this earthly world that will be judged in the 'afterlife'. This is a core, integral part of the faith. In many Muslim families it is drummed in through the theology of Islam, allied to a sense of mysticism around the after-life, and it is a common belief held by many Muslims that changing from the 'one true faith' to Christianity would be to turn away from God Himself to a blasphemous Trinity which worships man. On the bottom rung of the ladder in the eyes of the majority of believing Muslims, are those who leave Islam and do not believe in God at all; they will be eternally damned, as though their soul has no route for salvation and there is only one route, towards an eternity of torture, fire and castigation.

There simply is no middle ground here and this is why many people who lose their belief in Islam or choose to leave Islam and turn towards atheism, for example, do not share their beliefs within their families. The impact on both the individual and family members is usually substantive, with the rest of the family feeling that they are somehow responsible for the loss of faith in their loved one. A collective sense of pain, shame, fear and anger also grows within the family, meaning that even in 2018, it is still extremely difficult for some Muslims to say that they have lost faith in Islam and to abandon faith for a belief that what we see, hear and experience in this world, is what the beauty of life is about and that spirituality is a way of expressing our own fears and insecurities.

In compiling this book, our aim is that the voices that are not heard should be heard, since the vast majority of Muslims are people who have compassion and care at the heart of their beliefs. Yet, the only voices we seem to hear from within Muslim communities are those who seek to reinforce their singular interpretation of Islam, whilst some Muslim campaigning groups bully, intimidate and malign liberal voices and dissenters within Islam. Like thugs in the night, they spread fear, smear, and whip up a social media smokescreen, endangering anyone they cannot control or who questions their perception of Islam. Like clerics undertaking an Inquisition, they use anything deemed by them to be an insult against Islam, to delegitimise dissenting voices.

Therefore, in the UK today, liberal voices within Islam are being heard less as Muslims increasingly feel fear and are embattled from Islamophobic incidents and from the effects of a US President in the White House, who seemingly thinks that retweeting material from far-right campaigners like Jayda

Fransen does not have global and real-world psychological impacts. The growing sense of fear within Muslim communities is creating a turning inward and feelings of deep anger within Muslim communities, meaning that the space to question elements of the faith or challenge centuries-old orthodoxy is being shut down because of intimidation and thuggery from external forces. When a community feels fear, the first people it often turns against, are those co-religionists who are seen to be 'non-conformists'. This book is our attempt to give people of Muslim heritage the space to discuss their ideas and beliefs and to provide us with an insight into why they choose to leave Islam. We acknowledge that the issues facing the authors of this book are not unique to former Muslims.

In fact, one of the editors, Aliyah Saleem, co-founded the organisation Faith to Faithless and successfully integrated it into the British national charity Humanists UK. Aliyah attended an Islamic boarding school in Britain and Pakistan where she was training to become an Islamic scholar. Aliyah has spoken publicly about the draconian Islamic school rules that were imposed on her (and others) after publicly coming out as an apostate. She has campaigned for a national conversation about faith schools and the issue of apostasy. Faith to Faithless works with people from a range of religious and cult backgrounds and raises awareness about the discrimination that apostates face.

The conversation surrounding this issue has been highly polemical and largely theological in nature. Workers within Faith to Faithless are told about personal experiences that have come about because of horrific prejudice against apostates that makes it virtually impossible for such people to live authentic and open lives, even in Britain. It has been argued by many Muslim leaders that blasphemy and apostasy laws exist in other parts of the world because of the misinterpretation of ancient religious texts. Whether there is a true interpretation of Islam or not, the prejudice against people who have no faith is very real and it has led to the deaths of some people within Muslim majority countries. It has also led to an ambivalence and apathy from Muslims, many of whom see apostates or those accused of blasphemy, as having brought it upon themselves. In the end, can we truly say that in Muslim majority countries, people who leave Islam are physically, emotionally or psychologically safe from harm? We would wish that answer to be yes, but in fact we do not see that point being reached within the next two to three generations.

As you will see, this book is both about and not about Islam. We understand that there are countless interpretations of Islamic scripture and it can be argued that there are as many versions of Islam as there are Muslims. Religion is not only a set of Scriptures; it is a way of life and a way of understanding the world. Each region of the world has its own type of Islam, moulded by local history, politics and culture. This book is an attempt to bring to the surface extremely marginalised and oppressed voices within Muslim communities, voices which have been neglected or deliberately stamped out, in the hope that we can challenge stereotypes and move closer to social cohesion. Apostates are viewed as 'traitors', 'native informants', 'stupid' and 'dangerous', simply for living their own lives how they want. They are judged just because they do not conform and their standing in society regarded as fair game to malign, branded as many are as 'Islamophobes' and 'Muslim haters'. Such abuse is the denial of the basic concept of human rights, where people can choose to believe in what they want and to live their lives free from fear and with dignity.

Professional commentators and self-appointed community leaders may pacify audiences by saying that the 'true' Islam is not reflected in hatred towards others shown by their co-religionists, but the fact remains that there are family relationships being torn apart by deeply-held and little-understood prejudice. Many who turn away from Islam suffer isolation; many have been thrown out of their homes, face punitive fines, even the death penalty, and fear being threatened with legal action for posts on social media platforms such as Facebook or Twitter. Raif Badawi, who was accused of insulting Islam, has never publicly renounced the faith, yet he is lying in a Saudi prison cell while his family wait anxiously for his release. Badawi was arrested in 2012 and was charged with 'insulting Islam through electronic channels'. He was also charged with apostasy, leading to his conviction in 2013 and a decade long sentence with a thousand lashes attached to the imprisonment.

It is important to understand that the issue of freedom of expression is not one that only affects former Muslims. The accusation of apostasy has long been used against non-orthodox, liberal and reformist Muslims, but in today's climate, those self-appointed moral guardians who whip up social media storms against co-religionists seeking to question Islam, or against those who leave Islam, are putting at risk the lives of those they attack. It is as simple as that. The brutal murder of Glasgow shopkeeper Asad Shah in March 2016 by Bradford-based Tanveer Qadri, shows that people are willing to kill in the belief that they are defending and protecting Islam from ideas, words and comments on social media. Qadri drove from Bradford to Glasgow having come across online social media postings from Shah. According to Qadri, Shah's postings that he was a Prophet catapulted him to take action, no doubt led by a desire to harm the innocent and harmless shopkeeper since he was seen by Qadri to be blaspheming against Islam and against Muhammad, the Prophet of Islam. Such intolerance, including the whipping up of campaigns by Islamist groups in the United Kingdom in the 'defence' of Islam because another Muslim holds an alternative view, must be challenged at every step. We cannot tolerate a culture of fear and silence within any faith, nor can we allow anyone to feel so intimidated that they cannot speak out for fear of the religious ultra-right in Islam whipping up a storm against them on social media for merely stating an alternative. The murder of Asad Shah should be a wake-up call for all of us who believe in dialogue and in the betterment of society through the exchange of ideas.

It is clear that we have a real challenge on our hands with those who defend faith by overtly or covertly promoting intimidation, fear and the development of a mob mentality, and who should be given no quarter in our country. We need to actively challenge any groups who believe they have the moral authority to make the lives of others miserable in retribution for challenging religious beliefs. For many Muslims, Islam is the one and true path and they see themselves as fortunate for being born into it. Those who challenge Islam can be viewed as pariahs; they are 'against' Islam and therefore to be viewed as the enemy within. Liberals in the West have found it difficult to navigate this conversation as they try to protect and work with Muslims who are also seen by those outside Islam as the enemy within. Fiyaz Mughal, the co-editor of this book, has worked extensively to support Muslims who face racism and anti-Muslim hatred from the far-right, and created the first national anti-Muslim hate crime monitor through a project called Tell MAMA. He has also challenged extremist Islamist preachers and groups in Britain and consequently suffered threats from people on both sides who call for division and segregation. Far right and Islamist activists and sympathisers have joint common cause in attacking those who believe in a society that is based on liberal principles and who have defended the human rights of all communities.

Six years of work, founding Tell MAMA, helping to shape social policy so that anti-Muslim hatred is taken seriously and influencing policy changes at Governmental levels, has not stopped attacks from both far right anti-Muslim haters and far right religious Islamists. The former seek to caricature all Muslims as the enemy and the latter seek to defend a view of Islam which they alone believe they can define, creating 'enemies within' by attacking liberals, reformers and all Muslims who do not share their sectarian and polarised worldviews. We also understand and acknowledge that racists often use the examples of Muslims who have left the faith as grenades to launch at Muslim communities. This has muddied the waters and led to liberal activists not only remaining silent about the prejudices that affect apostates, but sometimes also attacking them from a misplaced sense of protectiveness towards Islam. The conflation of criticism of Islam and of individual Muslims has made this conversation even more difficult to have. We believe that through exposure, representation and offering a safe space for people to speak, we can challenge the prejudices that are tearing our communities apart. There are social solutions available to us that do not necessarily require reform to implement.

Islam, like other faiths, has a rich history of pluralism, introspection, self-criticism at historical junctures, and times of literalism. It has its liberal and conservative thinkers, its rebels and its giant personalities who have moved mountains to create social change. Yet, since the Iranian revolution in 1979, Islam (in this case Shia Islam, which has been placed centrally by theologians in Iran as the driving force behind the overthrow of the Shah), created the scene for Islam to be associated with revolt and militarism. This was followed within years by the Lebanese 'suicide bombings' which became part of the Lebanese civil war and which tore apart Lebanon in the mid-1980s. News agencies globally carried pictures of young bearded men wearing green or black headbands carrying Islamic inscriptions and preparing to launch suicide attacks on military positions, be they Israeli army or Christian Maronite. Many of these suicide attacks were filmed so that they could be used to 'inspire' young men and women in the refugee camps in Lebanon, to kill others as if doing this meant they would have an easy route to heaven. Martyrdom, it seemed, was now a business of killing anything and anyone deemed to be a threat to the sectarian and religious zealots who ran extortion rackets in Lebanon at the time.

No faith community came out clean from the brutality of the Lebanese war, but the actions of these suicide bombers, further reinforced the links between Islam and violence in the public consciousness. The Iran-Iraq War, which lasted eight years, saw Libya's Colonel Muammar Gaddafi, use Islam when it suited him to rouse Muslim communities in his anti-American outbursts. Similarly, the war in Afghanistan which saw the Russians leave the country with little dignity after being defeated by a religiously motivated set of guerrillas, also placed Islam within the bracket of its association with violence. Picture after picture beamed globally showed young Muslim men, carrying Kalashnikovs, shooting at targets and shouting out the name of God (Allah), with a passion. Since 9/11 and the attacks on the United States, the rise of the Taliban, Al-Qaeda and its offshoots, Daesh or Islamic State, Al-Shabaab and many other horrific examples of Islam's hijacking and abuse to validate violence against many across the globe, the faith has become synonymous with violence and blind rage. To many, including some Muslims, Islam is in a state of flux and in a state of deterioration, meaning that many will leave it over time and choose to espouse no faith at all, or will convert to another.

Put simply, you cannot continue to buy into a brand that has been so damaged over decades, before you give up purchasing and standing up for it. It is basic human nature that some will defend their belief and their brand identity, since it is a fundamental part of their character, while others will make a choice to move on and many others will simply go quiet and seek solace in a variety of different ways. What is taking place today – this fissure, split and segmentation within Muslim communities – means that over the next fifty years the numbers leaving the faith behind will continue to rise, and those leaving will continue to be discriminated against if we do not have a frank and honest conversation about this issue. This book aims to offer a way in to that conversation.

The first step is to build bridges between the nonreligious and religious communities. The editors of this book are an example of what can be produced and achieved by putting our differences aside and working together for the betterment of oppressed people in our society who are pressurised in various ways to conform. The authors in this book come from different backgrounds and they offer a valuable insight into the lived reality of being a Muslim and going through the journey of leaving their faith behind. You will see that the lazy stereotypes about apostates, including the assertion that they never truly understood Islam, is challenged by the inclusion of authors who have followed Islam for a long time, and dedicated years of their lives to its formal study. It was difficult to find female former Muslims who would openly write about their experiences, because there is an additional layer of difficulty for women who wish to leave their faith behind. We have included two anonymous accounts from formerly Muslim women, including one who still conceals her true beliefs from her family. For many former Muslim women, to leave Islam in their minds is not enough as they are still expected to follow the Islamic gender norms that are expected of them, particularly regarding dress and marriage. When some women leave Islam, they still might wear the Islamic dress and be visibly Muslim either due to social pressure or actual force, or to not arouse suspicion.

It is therefore our hope that this book leads to wider

discussions about how faith communities and those who reject faith can listen to each other's experiences with some empathy. Right now, we believe that unless that step is taken, important voices will be drowned out and lives will continue to be damaged because of a prejudice that has already claimed many voiceless people, people whose names will now never be known to us.

LIBERAL FALL-BACK – THE ASSAULT ON LIBERALISM

FIYAZ MUGHAL

It has been a journey, one that feels like it has taken many lifetimes rolled into one. A rollercoaster of elation, belonging and security, to one of vulnerability and feeling alone, yet I am quietly confident that there is truth in my experiences.

My desire to give a voice to those who have left faith comes from a place of deep introspection, of fear, and a real desire to explore what God and belief in one deity, or indeed many, really means. I may not be able to describe the latter, but I can certainly try to do the former.

For most of my life, there was an automatic, almost reflex, reaction where God was part of my life, as a Muslim and as someone with deeply-held socio-liberal beliefs. I protected my faith and held onto the belief that God needed my defence, that he had given me life and the least that I could do was to defend him when people abused him, and in particular, when they abused him by abusing Islam.

Yet, it had not always been like this. My defence of Islam and God really came into being when I came to the UK, having spent my childhood in East Africa and been brought up in British expatriate schools. Which religion I belonged to never seemed to be a problem in Kenya and faith was a part of the lives of the vast majority of people there, be they Christian, Sikh, Hindu, Muslim or animist. The 'faith fault-lines' were only felt when I came to the UK in 1983, and they have been buffeting me since then. It seemed that in Africa what faith you were from was not a problem, yet in the UK I could feel an almost tangible difference, both as an Asian male and as a Muslim.

Having been schooled and educated within Jesuit and Christian schools in Africa in my childhood, God taking the form of a human being seemed obvious and had been inculcated in me through the story of God creating Adam in his own image, a very Christian version of the manifestation of God. Yet, as I have grown older, the thought of an omnipotent God, leading my life and having written my experiences for me, seems distant. Such beliefs provide strong re-assurances for many Muslims throughout the world and have deeply shaped the fundamentals of Islam; that what is 'written' (by the Almighty), is meant to be, as though human being have no control over the situations in which we find ourselves. It is therefore an over-riding narrative within Islam and deeply held by Muslims generally, that they should throw their worries and their anxieties to the winds and into the palms of the Almighty.

This belief that 'what is written will happen' provides reassurance to many Muslims globally, and provides certainty in an increasingly uncertain world. It is something that still provides me with comfort in a way, though there is also a part of me that realises that the decisions we make ourselves are the ones that shape our lives. The spiritual and the rational do not so much conflict as accommodate each other, as and when needed, to make sense of a world that is so fast-changing and often confusing.

Many who read this, and who have been brought up within faith, will feel these words and believe them, as they render themselves and their futures to God. Yet tomorrow, they will wake up and make decisions that will alter and shape their future actions and their experiences. This dichotomy is what many of us live with, and they balance a reality with the belief in what is unseen.

There is something within us all that seeks comfort and stability, whether it is through belief in faith or through belief in science and rationality. In fact, these routes that are driven by a desire to make order out of the chaos of life, are a natural part of the human psyche and of our need to feel in control of our lives. They are a reaction to an innate sense of fear that is part of the human psyche and biology, a throwback to the risks that humans faced as they lived in the open and where threats to their lives were constantly all around them.

We cannot just put aside something that is inherent within us. It is a desire to believe in something beyond our own control that can provide solace and comfort and reduce the anxieties and fears that arise from life. A thousand years ago, these fears were probably based on physical threats due to a lack of safety, while today the pressures of a fast-moving world throw up other insecurities to which we are struggling to adapt.

For some, the concept of God and faith has little relevance to their lives and seems an out-dated framework of belief patterns. They see it as a means of control, self-limitation, moribund and irrelevant to modern lifestyles. For billions of others, they cannot imagine their lives without it and feel palpable fear when they are forced to think that there may be no God. God is for them like taking a calming drug, sometimes with no side effects, while for others it skews their outlook on life, blurs their vision towards others and divides communities. The former may have health benefits; the latter certainly has the potential to start wars and escalate conflict and terrorism, the scourge that is affecting so many countries.

Hearing the voices of those who leave faith

The voices of people who have left faith increasingly need to be heard since they speak of experiences and beliefs that are neither morally different nor heretical. They are based on their value judgements and their sense of meaning.

My decision to co-edit and author this book comes from the firm belief that those who do not believe in faith or who reject it, are not morally inferior to those who go to church every week or those who pray five times a day. Morality does not come in the form of belief in God, even though faith has created a moral framework for billions of people. It lies in the way people lead their lives, how they care for others and how they treat them.

We don't have to believe in God to be moral people. This should go without saying; however, many people still believe the two go hand in hand and that one cannot exist without the other. That is not the case.

Some have therefore chosen to attack the concept of faith and the belief in an unseen, all-powerful deity. Many, who have left faith, feel anchored and secure believing that this life is what they have, and they have chosen to live it to the full. There are increasing numbers of ex-Muslims who reject Islam and any form of faith since they see terrorism voiced in the name of Islam and have experienced negative life events, driven, in their eyes, by the influence of religion on their parents, friends or relatives.

Whatever the truth, the fact is that some of those who have chosen to leave faith have done so because the dogma and doctrinal issues of the faith that they were born into clashed head-on with their sense of identity, rationality, common sense and in some cases, their dignity. For others, it became restrictive, forceful, constraining and dangerous to them. What was supposed to provide a sense of identity, belief, security and solace, became a prison that locked them mentally into a place of pain, fear and anxiety. This loss of personal control, for some, led to mental and physical crises, some of which they still suffer to this day as they seek to re-establish control over their lives.

What we are seeing is that for some, their sense of identities and beliefs are fluid and becoming increasingly more fluid in the world in which we live. Choices are made and rejected, in a way that would have been unthinkable just three or four decades ago. Part of the reason that people have the chance to make those choices is that they can do so without significant fear to their lives and with legal protections. Allied to this have been changing social attitudes and the liberalisation of society's norms.

Even within the faith into which I was born, Islam, the chances of an ex-Muslim being killed for leaving the faith are very low in the United Kingdom, but that is not to say that they will not be subjected to rejection from their immediate family, to psychological pressures or abuse. Some of this sort of treatment I have also seen within families born into Christian traditions where one member of the family converts to Islam. There are psychological pressures, cycles of emotional abuse and the shunning of individuals as punishment for their decision to convert to Islam. So, I know that such issues are not unique to Islam.

In countries like Pakistan and Egypt, abusing, leaving or changing faith can have violent and deadly consequences. Blasphemy laws in Pakistan have led to the violent deaths and imprisonment of people deemed to have insulted Muhammad or Islam. In Pakistan, even the mere accusation of insulting the faith can lead to mob justice and violent murder. Faith has been weaponised by successive Governments to mobilise the population and to play to a sense of macho-nationalism. The strategy has been to focus the people's attention on external threats through religio-nationalism, whilst corruption, nepotism and obfuscation have become synonymous with Government.

This deflection has meant that anyone who goes against the grain of religion is seen as a threat to the state itself, because faith and the state have become entirely intertwined. No wonder so many people rarely dissent in such circumstances. The results have been devastating, with strong support for extremist groups in Pakistan and Afghanistan, where literalism and absolutism within Islam have become the norm.

The possibility for people to change, whether they change faith or reject faith completely and take on a new identity, is part of the human spirit and something that makes us unique. However, that change can only take place in an environment where people are free to make those decisions without a threat to their lives. It is also one of the reasons why I pushed to make this book happen. Changing identity is part and parcel of life and we should not fear it, but embrace it, just as much as we embrace the freedom to choose other aspects of how we live our lives.

Faith versus fear

One of the things which those who have left faith have said to me, is that they have felt a strong desire to slough off their previous attachment to the faith they were born into or which they practised, and to find a community of ex-believers. Some have joined ex-Muslim groups, whilst others have gone on to be critical voices against Islam and even against Muslims, in their total rejection of all things Islam and Muslim. In a similar cycle to new converts to Christianity or Islam, their zealotry about their new beliefs tapers off as time passes and gradually resets itself, as they grow into their new-found identity as people who have left faith behind. This 'resetting' is important, as it means that many learn to accept the change in their lives, without blaming those who continue to be followers of a faith or seeking to take away their right to be Muslims.

I have worked with gay Muslims who have been unable to reconcile Islam with their sexuality. The story of Lot, reflecting Biblical traditions, is one reference in the Quran which infers that homosexuality is against God's will. This one reference has spawned millennia of homophobia – though Muslim majority communities have overlooked homosexuality during times when these communities have been ruled by liberal elites and when they felt no risk from external pressures or threats. The founder of the Mughal Empire in India, Babur, is also reported to have been in love with another man[1] and at points, the Mughal Empire turned a blind eye and even celebrated sexuality in vivid and graphic form, showing its ease with sexuality.

Yet, even with gay Muslim communities which span every Muslim majority country in the world, as do LGBTQ communities within every nation across the globe, why is there an unwillingness to talk in the wider community about the differences within them? Why is there the refusal to recognise that the diversity of such communities is actually a part of their strength and why instead has conformity become the rallying call for the loudest voices in these communities – a bit like General Custer holding the straggling vestiges of his troops on Last Stand Hill. This conformity which hinders re-interpretation of Islamic text and a reflection of the context in which Islamic events took place, is damaging the faith and driving people away from it. It is also creating a false sense of identity, as though insisting that people cannot be gay and Muslim, or that people cannot identify as being ex-Muslim, forcing people to dissociate with this element of their past as in order to 'protect the faith'.

This entrenchment has grown within some sections of

[1] http://www.pinknews.co.uk/2013/12/17/author-homophobia-came-into-india-not-homosexuality/

British Muslim communities. This is partly as a reaction to global events such as the 'War on Terror' and global terrorism causing increased anti-Muslim hatred, hatred which has led some to try to draw a veil over the pluralism within their communities. Those who shout the loudest are often British Muslims of Pakistani heritage who rarely speak about Black British Muslims of African heritage, nor those from the Balkans, Central Asia or the Caucasus. This centralised sub-continent lens of Islam is the one around which the loudest voices and websites congregate and issue their clarion call.

So, as some choose to leave Islam, there arise more vocal calls for the defence of Islam within sections of Muslim communities. With regard to sexuality, the response from these websites, defending their narrow view of Islam, is that no one who is gay can be Muslim, as though over the last 1400 years of Islam's existence, not a single Muslim has been gay. These groups and individuals accept the notion that if someone professes that there is no God but (the one) God, and Muhammad is his messenger, then he or she is a Muslim. There are supposedly no more questions asked if this is said of their own free will and without their being under pressure or having any mental incapacity. But in reality, if a gay person wants to make this commitment, because of their sexuality, their acceptability would be called into account, as though Islam were developed in thought, mind and spirit only by heterosexuals. Such entrenched, illogical fear has turned some people away from Islam in the United Kingdom, where instead of acknowledgement and acceptance, they have been met with resentment, hatred and intolerance. This is not just unique to Islam, but it is prevalent within large sections of Muslim communities in the UK as though faith and belief remain the same over time. They do not remain constant, nor do they evolve in a predictable way.

Many who have left Islam and turned away from Muslim

communities, have been women who felt restricted and constricted by cultural pressures dressed up as Islamic norms. Issues of 'izzet', or honour, which are mainly culturally based in the sub-continent, have led them to feel hemmed or closed in and unable to express themselves. These feelings do not come about because of one incident; they take hold through a combination of incidents building over time and eventually reaching a breaking point. They are mixed with a rising animosity and a series of grievances against the people and the beliefs that are causing them. Sadly, Islam is one of the factors that has been cited as the cause of their distress. While one might disagree that Islam constricts women's growth and development, I know that in many cases, parents have misused Islam and faith to curtail and restrict activities that they do not agree with. Instead of talking and engaging with their children, some parents use faith as a means of morally pressuring their daughters, or making them compliant and controlling them, as though the honour of the family is tied up with a young woman's sexual organs. It seems that in some cases, basic parenting is less about communication and more about punishments and pressure. Fear it seems, has been the modus operandi for some parents, and in turn it has driven their children away from them and from the faith into which they were born.

We also need to look at those who have had faith overshadow every aspect of their lives, as though the only aspect of their identity was being Christian or Muslim. Later in this book you will hear the words of my co-author and co-editor Aliyah Saleem as she shares her own experience of this, one that cannot be easily brushed aside. Possessing a detailed Islamic knowledge and having been schooled within Islamic educational institutions, she left the faith at the age of 19 and does not believe in a God or omnipotent being. In a recent interview[2] with a local newspaper, she stated, 'I studied at fundamentalist schools from the age of about 11 and I was quite indoctrinated in a way that most Muslims in the UK are not. Science, reason, evolution, and feminism were factors in me coming to a place where I no longer could see Islam as the one true religion. I found that my understanding of Islam contradicted my newly emerging feminist outlook and I could not reconcile faith with it.'

Aliyah spent six years in Islamic religious institutions, including a year in Pakistan at the Al-Hudaa Institute for Muslim women, the same institution where Tafsheen Malik,[3] one-half of the San Bernardino killers, studied. Tafsheen Malik studied at the women only religious school in Pakistan, known for its puritanical interpretations of Islamic theology, between 2013 and 2014. Malik's actions with her husband, Syed Rizwan Farook, led to the deaths of 14 people and 22 more injured as the couple sprayed bullets into the Inland Regional Centre in San Bernardino, California, after they gave their allegiance to Abu Bakr Al-Baghdadi on social media.

Aliyah wore the hijab and the jilbab (a long body covering) from the age of 11 and started to cover her hands by wearing gloves when she was at the Al-Hudaa Institute in Pakistan. She often speaks about how she would also berate her friends at the time for wearing hijabs and body coverings that were not black in colour and her outlook on life was rigid and brittle. This rigidity rubbed up against Aliyah's innate sense that there was more to her that wanted to be expressed. She talks about her desire to read and to devour as much information as she could during

[2] http://www.plymouthherald.co.uk/how-i-turned-my-back-on-islam-and-became-an-atheist-campaigner/story-29855803-detail/story.html

[3] https://www.thetimes.co.uk/article/aliyah-saleems-life-at-the-islamic-womens-institute-khrs6xz0ssh

this period of her life and how as she read more, the enforced religious claustrophobia slowly started to melt away.

We know that within many religious communities, this enforced religious rigidity is imposed upon women, mixed in with a desire to protect the 'izzet' of families and communities where women are still seen as the means of maintaining respect within the wider community. This is not just taking place in Yemen or the Arabian Peninsula. It is happening in the United Kingdom, where instead of Islam being interpreted within families as a force for enhancing the rights of women, it is used by some to shame them and crush other aspects of their identities. This is unacceptable and within the Millennial generation that has more life choices than previous generations, it is inevitable that many more young Muslim women will reject the part of their identity that they feel constricts them, as they see other young people around them having a wider range of experiences.

Today, travelling through parts of Birmingham, Bradford or Manchester, the overt religiosity of Muslim women has perhaps become more visible than ever. Yet, just 30 years ago, during the early 1980s when I was growing up, such overt religiosity was not present in Muslim communities. This phenomenon is caused by more people espousing identity politics and a community feeling embattled and searching for its own identity in a rapidly changing and sometimes hostile world. None of this can be easy on young Muslims and motivates many to search for an identity that is exclusively Muslim and holds the promise of an Islamic utopia beyond the bounds of the United Kingdom. We have seen the consequences of that, as hundreds of young British Muslims have left the country and sought sanctuary and solace in the barbarity of the so-called Islamic State (IS). Some have been duped by the slick propaganda of IS, while others have been drawn to its violence, its promotion of Islam as an all-empowering and conquering force and holding the promise of the sense of community they feel is missing in the United Kingdom. This sense of fracture, of dislocation of self and a feeling of being lost in a rapidly changing world, will no doubt, lead to many young people either embracing their faith more strongly, or in some instances, rejecting it, whether that be through a vocal ideological rejection, or more quietly, perhaps including changing their name and behaviour.

Islamism versus Islam

There are those who have rejected Islam because of the phenomenon of Islamism, an intrusive, political, all-encompassing supremacist belief that the political and social world must be delivered in line with Islamic principles and that democratic structures are a threat to such a guiding social framework. Resurgent because of the failure of pan-Arab nationalism, military defeats in the Middle East, the Iranian revolution and the successful ejection of Russia from Afghanistan in the 1980s, Islamism has created a stifling environment where dissent is rejected and seen as a threat and where there is little tolerance of dissenters. Algeria in the 1990s, Morsi's Egypt, and Iran, stand out as examples of environments where Islamist movements fared no better in changing the political and social environments they sought to challenge, in some cases becoming as oppressive as the regimes they opposed.

Islamist activities in the Middle East in the 1980s and 1990s quickly spread to the United Kingdom, because of a range of factors, including Islamist campaigners seeking asylum in the UK as they fled from Egypt, Libya, Saudi Arabia and other countries in the Maghreb and the Arabian Peninsula. What they found was many Muslim communities that were reliant mainly on institutions that were founded on principles of the Muslim

Brotherhood and where Islamism had become synonymous with Islam. This was even more acute after the *Satanic Verses* affair of 1989, a controversy that further polarised Muslims and reinforced the Islamic and Muslim identity of many at the time. Written by Salman Rushdie and published by Penguin, *The Satanic Verses* could be read as the spiritual, psychological and physical journey of immigrants who find themselves in a social and cultural limbo, having left the culture that they grew up in and having to integrate into one with very different social and cultural norms. But it was a sequence in the book that questioned the revelations by Muhammad and which cast the Prophet's wives as being prostitutes, that caused the furore and demonstrations led by Muslim communities at the time.

The influence of Islamists deeply affected both the practice of Islam and its politicisation. The Islam practised by first and second generation Muslim migrants to the United Kingdom had been transformed into a politically reactionary Islam, at a time when institutions and organisations representing the views and needs of British Muslims were growing. *The personal* had become *the political* and a new generation of Muslims was exposed to Islamist views and opinions as though they were normal; local activities and events by some groups regularly promoted views that Muslims were 'under threat' and that Islam was 'under attack'. The peaceful, deeply introspective and reflective nature of Islam was being overshadowed by angry, politicised and reactive responses of a younger generation of Muslims who saw Islam not as a personal belief system, but a way of life that others must follow. Therein lay the problem which was to see third and fourth generation Muslims berate their parents and relatives for being 'bad Muslims' and for being corrupted by the 'decadence of the West'. I personally know of cases post 9/11, where small groups of Islamist extremists, no older than 20 years of age, would turn up to mosques in the Midlands and humiliate imams after prayer, including those who could speak fluent English. Islam for them, had moved from the personal to the political and out to the extreme fringes.

Islamist victimisation and the threat of imminent conflict is no different to the poison peddled by far-right extremist groups. Both groups believe that conflict is inevitable, and that Muslims and non-Muslims cannot live and co-exist peaceably together. Such groups believe that they are victimised and wear the badge of victimisation with pride. They believe in a future where there is no accommodation of the 'other'. Islamists identify the 'other' as non-Muslims and non-believers and for far-right groups it is anyone who is deemed to be a 'foreigner', 'migrant' or 'Muslim'. It is this campaign of victimisation and 'othering' that is turning some young people away from Islam and is why it is necessary to disentangle Islamism from Islam.

Now some may say that Islam is all-encompassing, and that Islamism is Islam. Islam is indeed a blueprint for people to lead their lives, and we are lucky that in the United Kingdom all that is needed to live as a Muslim is available. Halal food, mosques, Islamic burials and workplace accommodation for religiosity, are all examples of opportunities available for someone to follow their faith, and many of these are not available in Europe. The accommodation of different faiths is one of the endearing and somewhat unique elements of the culture of the United Kingdom, a principle that says: you can worship who and how you want as long as you follow the law and do not fall foul of it. This principle, it has to be said, was also one that Rome implemented in its colonies and within the heart of its Empire. However, this personal freedom does not extend to enforcing on others one's personal religious beliefs, something which is at the heart of Islamism, not Islam.

Some of those who have left Islam also talk about being unable to reconcile the modern world with views and values that they have come across within their families. Views about the rights of women, minorities, those who reject faith and the use of force or violence are clearly laid out within Islam and have been debated for over a thousand years within Muslim communities and these discussions, like life in general, have never been static or predictable. The failure of Islamic religious leaders in the United Kingdom to frame these discussions within a Western context in a way that is relevant to the country has meant that a gulf has opened up between some young people and a modern understanding of such issues within Islam. To date, there are no coherent narratives to have come out from the vast amount of historical information within Islamic traditions.

A handful of imams have tried to frame these discussions within the current context, but they have never gained much traction, and as Imam Mamadou Bocoum[4] says, 'new interpretations' of the Quran are needed. Bocoum has also repeatedly talked about the need for a 'Fish and Chips' form of Islam; in other words, an Islam that is anchored within a British context. He also has stated that Islamic theologians need to look within the West, not towards the East to find the roots of Islam that reflect a human-rights based culture, which he insists, is within the heart of the faith. In fact, it is this 'British Islam' that Bocoum promotes, that was the cornerstone of his mentor, the late great Zaki Badawi,[5] the first person to explain and contextualise the importance and the relevance of it. Badawi went on to found the Muslim College, which was his attempt at producing a British Islam that reflected the context, norms and values of the country.

We also should not look away when the bullying and intimidation by Islamist groups in the UK attempts to try to

[4] https://www.thetimes.co.uk/article/mamadou-bobouc-koran-needs-new-interpretation-to-help-fight-terror-0jfgpmllz

[5] http://www.independent.co.uk/news/obituaries/zaki-badawi-6110603.html

stop people discussing and re-interpreting what Islam means to them. WhatsApp, email and web-based campaigns attempt to delegitimise those who dissent and who speak out against some practices within Islam that they feel are regressive, that are associated with cultures that have built up around Islam, or that go against their natural instincts. This is not to single out Islam as the only faith in which this happens, though the intimidation and the fear instilled by such Islamist groups need to be challenged by a chorus of voices which is very slowly building in strength and numbers over time. If people cannot speak up and explore faith and what it means to them, and in some cases, how it is irrelevant to their lives, then there is something fundamentally wrong in our society and the alarm bells should be ringing loud and clear for us all. Have no doubt that a suppression of more progressive voices in Islam means that the victim narrative pushed so hard by Islamist groups will continue to resonate within the minds of some young people.

Without a doubt, such attacks against dissenters in Islam show a weakness in those who seek to protect the faith. A belief system does not need protection, it needs debate, discussion and dialogue to keep it alive and more importantly, relevant. This idea of protectionism, as though God requires protection from debate, is no longer persuasive these days, when people have access to information at the touch of a button. Suppression of debate and dissent may have had a comforting effect for migrant Muslim communities when they were first in the UK in the 1960s and 1970s, since migration usually leads populations to hang on more tightly to their personal identities in a foreign country. However, Muslims have now been in the UK for more than 50 years, and they are no longer migrants or foreigners. They are part and parcel of the fabric of the United Kingdom and knee-jerk reflexive actions to defend the faith are tiresome in an age of mass information, debate and critique of ideas.

The more defensive a faith becomes about criticism or dissent, the greater the damage to that religious ideology in the long term. With such huge global changes afoot – partly driven by technology and access to information – cultural, social and religious boundaries are being torn apart, traditions re-assessed and faith and belief coming under significant critique. If these changes cannot be digested and processed by organised religious communities, then it is only a matter of time before they fragment under the changes that are taking place at a global level.

A culture of acceptance

Islam's history, like that of any faith, has been shaped by the political and civic world around it. Christianity, for example, had to adapt to fit a Greek-influenced Roman world when souls needed to be saved and when the apostles found themselves preaching to new audiences beyond Galilee and Jerusalem where Christianity was born. As did Islam, as it traversed through Arab audiences in the Arabian Peninsula and across the Maghreb. Its adaptation to local customs and cultures also took place northwards, eastwards, upwards and outwards across the Middle East, to the Indian subcontinent and into parts of modern-day China. Faith has therefore always adapted and been moulded by what it encounters and what surrounds it.

Such changes have also meant that at certain times in their history, faiths have gone through periods of enormous change, partly led by internal dissent or by the development of seats of learning that encouraged critical thinking or that questioned the idea of intellectual boundaries that could not be crossed.

Once again, for all of the ancient faiths in today's world, these processes would have taken place time and time again.

Islam repeatedly went through such cycles as universities from Cairo to Baghdad encouraged an enlightenment within Islam that took in exploration of the sciences, debate, critical thinking and on to translations of volumes of Greek philosophy. The latter were brought back into public consciousness through Arabic translations of these volumes and their integration into practical learning.

Such cycles ensured that faiths remained relevant to the times in which they found themselves, and this was a natural process, one that renewed or rejected elements within faiths. Yet, during the last five decades, Islamist movements in the UK have skilfully promoted the concept of blind faith, thereby suppressing any sense of disentangling the political from the spiritual, the cultural from the faith of Islam and the Wahhabi from the Sufi and more open and progressive forms of Islam. These changes are only taking place now and are mainly driven by Islamist extremism which has infiltrated and taken cancerous root in some sections of Muslim communities. It is only within the last decade that the Islamist hegemony is being pushed back, which is to be warmly welcomed, but there is no natural momentum building up. Any progress seems to stop and start, but nonetheless, a change is taking place.

In the end, I contend that Islamist movements have hijacked the faith of Islam in their desire for political gain, and, in doing so, have done immeasurable damage to the reputation of this great faith. They have made it brittle when it was never meant to be, used force and threats to maintain their hold over the faith and written into it an intolerance of Christians and Jews that was fundamentally not a part of the faith. They have also taken the spiritual and made it into a set of practices which people must undertake, as though merely going through the motions of faith means that people naturally are happy and fulfilled.

The Hanif Kureishi generation

As stated previously, this exportation of Islamist thinking which also seeped into parts of British Muslim communities by virtue of Muslim Brotherhood activists and networks in the United Kingdom, shut down dissent and marginalised those who sought to develop platforms where people could debate Islam and what it meant to them. Yet, there was a brief window where second and third generation British Muslims had a chance to explore their identities on a wider scale rather than just being Asian or Muslims. That window came in the mid-1980s with several films that encapsulated the complex intersectionality of identities that were developing for young Asians and, more specifically, for young Muslim men.

Films written by Hanif Kureishi entitled *My Beautiful Laundrette* (1985) and *Sammy and Rosie Get Laid* (1987) explored hard and real-life issues of racism, isolation, sexuality, mixed-race relationships and racial violence in a Britain that was still trying to be at ease with itself and its minority communities. This frankness in film-making allowed mainly second generation British Asians of Pakistani heritage to explore the multiple identities they had and to explore life beyond the restrictive boundaries of being young boys who had to live up to ideals of 'no sex before marriage', 'religiosity' and being hard workers and achievers. The Hanif Kureishi generation started to see life through the prism of just being, rather than through the prism of identity politics, and many relished being in different kinds of relationships, living out a new part of who they were and crossing racial and faith boundaries through those relationships. It was a period of exploration and of imagination, of excitement and validation, of racism and racial solidarity as well as solidarity between minority groups. Those were heady days, times of pain, but times of hope.

Today, much of that spirit has been lost and I find young Muslims in their mid-twenties who lecture me, a 46-year-old man, about why I don't have a beard. I am lectured about why I should pray five times a day, why the West hates Muslims, how Prevent (the Government's community focussed counter-terrorism agenda) is used to spy on Muslims and how social progressives within Islam are a threat to the faith.

Why wouldn't things like this put off some who were born as Muslims? The enormous appetite of some media outlets to vilify Muslims as a whole, alongside Islamist online groups pouring out paranoia that the State is against Muslims and that your future is one of securitisation and harassment, have effects. The latter narrative is mainly made by Islamist groups who, as I have said before, have done a disservice to the many young Muslims who consume their corrosive, victim-driven narrative. The former can and should be challenged, and it is within the realm and capability of British Muslims to object vocally and vociferously when such headlines are aimed at selling papers and dividing communities.

What I am arguing is that Islamism has been a major turn off for many who were born Muslims, who feel they are British, and who cannot associate with groups who suggest that the lot of Muslims in the UK is one of being dispossessed and fed a diet of paranoia and hopelessness. In turning away from Islamist messages, some have wholeheartedly rejected Islam, showing how toxic these narratives and groups have become.

Leaving Islam

Leaving faith, whether that be Islam, Christianity or Judaism, means starting afresh to some extent. Circles of friends and relations within families may fracture permanently though, more and more, people will assert their choice to be part of a faith community or to leave it. The key point here though is *choice*.

A 'British Islam' is much needed and will develop over the next two to three decades. Its initial developments are taking place in the here and now, yet there will also be many who choose to simply walk away and turn their backs on this part of their lives.

The people featured in this book are examples of those who have chosen to leave Islam behind for a number of reasons, and their journeys shine a light not only on their personal experiences, but on the experiences of Muslims as a whole. These co-authors are balanced, grounded people who have made a choice for their lives and their experiences cannot be dismissed as those of people who know nothing about Islam. Some of them have studied and been part of it for many years. Others have felt that they have had enough of feeling demonised within the faith because they were 'different'. Each experience has been unique.

For me, as a Muslim who believes in a divine entity that created life, yet who also believes in evolution and in the inspiration of men such as Jesus and Muhammad, my only call is this: for those who read on, do so with an open mind and without fear or trepidation, for some of the most enlightening events are the ones that make us question the world around us, including who we are and what we believe in.

BREAKING THE SILENCE

ALIYAH SALEEM

I suppose it started with my first period. It was a frightening experience to find myself bleeding one day. Sure, I had heard about it during sex education during middle school but the horror of the real-life event was scarring. It was painful and gross. Shortly after this I was buying training bras, being told not to go near boys and that I was going to an Islamic boarding school. I was told that I was becoming a woman and that meant that I needed to change. The moment that I began to bleed inconveniently from my uterus, my life changed forever. I was what they called a 'tomboy'. I liked climbing trees, playing on my skateboard, and running around on the football pitch with the boys. I had earned my place among them as I was considered 'not girly'.

There was another side of me that I kept hidden much better. It was the part of me that used to sneak into my sisters' room to wear their make-up and made me fall in love with two Irish boys at school. I was eleven and completely besotted with both because they had floppy hair and soft brown freckles across their cheeks. I was obsessed with magic and computer games. I loved to speak to adults as I walked home, beamed as they called me a 'clever girl' and would ask to be given more tests at school. The great unexplored Universe was my passion and I would lie in the garden in the evenings staring at the stars wondering what it would be like to be out there.

When it was announced that I would be sent to boarding school for 'my own sake', my world stopped making sense. I think most boarding schoolers could sympathise with me when I say that I felt like I was being cast away and this weighed heavily on my young heart. I felt that I was being punished for being a girl who might do something to ruin the family's reputation like other female cousins whose names we weren't allowed to mention any longer because they had brought shame to the family. There was always an uncle or an auntie clutching at their chests in indignation about having daughters who disobeyed them.

Nottingham-based Jamia Al-Hudaa, Islamic residential college for girls' website developer marketed their site well enough for the news to reach London and spark the interest of my well-meaning and somewhat naïve and trusting mother. She presented the news to me as though she was giving me a gift, telling me that they would teach me how to behave, that I would become a scholar and that I would bring her so much joy.

I wonder how I could have turned out sometimes – a dignified and conservative married Aliyah Saleem with children, guarded from the ills of the world: alcohol, drugs and perhaps the greatest test of all – the wandering hands and eyes of lustful men. I could have been a real role model to Muslim girls but instead I have been told by some Muslims that I have chosen to do the devil's work for him and to be a pied piper leading woman to hell. I was trained and given the preparation to dedicate my life to the cause of spreading Islam peacefully and obeying Allah by worshipping him and being a good wife as well a role model to my well-raised children.

Instead of this, I have decided to take up a life of my own choosing, and to some it is a life of sinfulness. I listen to music, dance, travel alone, have relationships outside of marriage and wear whatever I want to wear. The fear that my ears will be filled with molten lead for listening to music is little more than a distant nightmare lingering on the edges of my memory. I often get asked if I am afraid of hell and the honest answer is no. It has been almost a decade since I can last remember ever becoming overcome with the crippling fear that a fundamentalist has when she thinks of the hell fire. It would bring me such panic, that I would often dig my nails into my skin when I would think of the sins and thought crimes that I had committed. Try as I might I could never stop myself thinking sexual thoughts, could not stop myself from wanting to listen to music or hold back the deeply suppressed wave of doubts that had been lurking deep inside me since I was a child. Later in this chapter, I will explore some of these in more detail.

I will tell you some stories that might help you understand how I got to this point, why I left fundamentalism behind and why I am comfortable here, living on the edge of many cultures and identities, knowing that I live what could be considered a scandalous and sinful life that might lead me to the gates of Hell. I will tell you about my lived experiences of Islam and, as for almost everyone else, it was not the perfect embodiment of Scripture. I will not be able to convince many of you that I have given a robust disproval of Islam – because I am not trying to. Unlike most Muslims, I have studied Islamic Scripture formally in detail, but one should not have to be a trained scholar to have doubt and then decide not to follow Islam.

I have learnt how to feel comfortable in my own skin and I hope that by sharing parts of my life story, I can help others to understand the hybridity of the experiences faced by people of Muslim heritage better. More challengingly though, I will try to help those of you who need it, to find the courage inside you that is necessary to live an authentic life without the most destabilising of emotions: shame.

Part 1: Childish questions

It took me until into my mid-teens to start believing in Allah. I believed in magic, the devil, and the power of the Mother Earth from a young age, but God felt like more like a myth. If I had had a choice in the matter, I think I would have taken up some form of paganism which favoured a Goddess. I feared the male Abrahamic God before I truly believed in him. God was like the bogeyman to me, or a Gollum hiding in the corner of bedrooms watching out for naughty children who disobeyed their parents and wanted to follow their own desires.

I never settled well during madrassa classes[1] after school because I found the lessons boring and the headscarf used to feel itchy around my neck. The mosque was a stuffy place, shoes scattered everywhere, women separated from the men by bossy aunties who were always ready to lay down the law if they saw a strand of hair trying to make an escape out of your scarf. One of my childhood Quran teachers once slapped me hard against the face for not wearing my scarf properly. She pulled me close to her by my ear so that my cheek was within an ideal range for the full force of her holy hand.

I did not know what jinns[2] were when I started boarding school at the age of eleven. My tears at being sent away had dried up as we drove up to the tall, dark, gothic buildings at the top of a small hill in Nottingham. There was a tall spire-like shape in the distance which I could see and I wondered what could be hidden inside. My father didn't want me to go this school and he

[1] After-school classes which often took place in mosques or people's homes where we were taught about Islam and how to read the Quran.

[2] According to most Islamic schools of thought, Jinns are beings made of smoke-less fire, who like human beings have free will and will be judged by Allah on the last day. According to the myths, they can possess and harm human beings.

was trying to hide his upset by making jokes and looking cheerful. He had spent much of the five-hour journey in mournful silence. I gave my mother a quick kiss and she left, believing she was making the sacrifice for my own good – like Abraham getting ready to give up Isaac for the chop.

I was placed in a bedroom with 10 other girls – some were crying and others were tucked up in tiny nighties, unsure of what they should do. I lay in bed quietly and looking out the window as I drifted off to sleep, I could have sworn I saw a group of tiny nuns carrying a cross as they climbed up the trees. I knew that it was the moon shining through the trees, however I still thought it was a spooky image. The next morning, I told one of my room mates and by the evening a full-blown mass hysteria had broken out about something called 'jinns'. It was explained to me by an 'older girl' (12 years old) who had been brought in to offer her expert opinion on the matter. Jinns are beings made from smokeless fire and they are like humans. They have free will and will be judged on the Day of Judgment. They can see us but we can't see them unless they want to be seen and they are dangerous to humans. I was beside myself with excitement.

Here was an opportunity to have some fun. So, when everyone was getting ready for bed, I told my roommates the story of my previous night-time ordeal in detail when I saw the jinns outside of the window. They listened in fear and fascination. The supervisor walked by, switched off the light at 9.30pm sharp and we all scurried off to bed. A few hours later a girl started screaming, 'A face, a face, she is looking at me with her bright shining, white face!' Another girl cried, 'Oh my god it is looking at her, help, help!'

Girls jumped out of their beds and began screaming at the top of their lungs. The supervisor came crashing down on us and switched on the lights in absolute shock. The first girl was cowering in fear pointing at a sports bag with a white football painted on the side which had obviously been mistaken for the white face of a malicious being made entirely of smokeless fire. I squealed with laughter and waited quietly for everyone to settle down as a tape-recorded recitation of the Quran began playing outside our room to soothe everyone, before falling asleep.

I didn't believe in Islam when I started Islamic boarding school and I didn't believe in jinns when I was told about them. Nobody at the time considered that it was even possible that an eleven-year-old raised by Muslims could not actually believe in Islam.

It didn't matter what they taught me or how many different teachers spoke about religion; to me it felt like something made up to stop me from breaking school rules. I had one mission in life then, and that was to enjoy myself as much as possible and to get expelled, so that meant I had to live on the wrong side of the law. Every rule, whether it was not being allowed to chew gum or not being allowed to wear nail polish, was enforced by divine Scripture according to whichever teacher or supervisor was telling me off. The school rules were made up as teachers went along and they were infinite. It was a soul-crushing, boring first year where I was constantly in trouble because I was desperate to leave the school and return to my life of spending time in the park and watching the Extreme Sports Channel. The old saying 'All work and no play makes Jack a dull boy' makes perfect sense to me. No music, no TV, no books about love, no games consoles, no park, no school trips, no boys – I missed boys – no books with swearing, no books with magic, no make-up, no nail polish, no talking to boys on the phone, no questioning of religion, no questioning of your parents, no questioning at all.

Jamia Al-Hudaa was a no man's land – literally. Men were not allowed past certain doors and gates. We stayed hidden away, always prepared to guard our chastity while within the confines of Jamia, covering our bodies and hair where a man could accidently come upon us – in the halls, playgrounds, corridors, and classrooms or anywhere that may have a CCTV camera close by that would be inspected by male security guards.

This didn't suit me at all. I wanted to run around the playground and play football. I didn't care about covering my short black hair – it meant nothing to me when I was eleven, so I couldn't understand all the kerfuffle about covering it. I didn't really ask questions to start off with – I just broke all the rules. I think I broke almost every school rule in the five years that I was there and did things that surely would warrant a rule once they knew that it was possible.

By the end of the first year, I had accepted that I was not going to be expelled; the head teacher had told me that because I wanted to leave, they would keep me no matter what I did. I was so furious with my family by then that I didn't want to go home, preferring to remain at school during holidays if possible.

I started asking questions loudly in my second year after I had turned twelve, such as why would God punish the devil. We were studying the story of Adam and Eve in our 'History' class. I reasoned that if the devil was a jinn, which is the Islamic view on it, then he would have had free will unlike the Angels, celestial robots, who lack the freedom to make their own choices. I told my teacher that I had sympathy for the devil and I felt like God needed the devil to have led Adam and Eve astray to carry out his dark plan to fill the hellfire with disbelievers.

My teacher said it was a 'childish question' that was silly, not even worth answering.

I was bullied and called a Satanist for asking this. Even now, I can't help but respect Iblis,[3] the devil's courage – he stood his ground, spoke his mind and he made a valid point when he asked

[3] In Islamic theology, Iblis is the equivalent or Lucifer or the devil however unlike in Christian theology, he is believed to be jinn, a smokeless being who was originally on earth and then he was elevated to live with the angels in heaven because he was so pious.

why he should bow down to Adam, who is made of clay when he, the devil is made of smokeless fire. I sympathised. I wouldn't want to bow down to some random new creation just because he had learnt some words and was kind of aware of what was happening. Instead of answering the devil's question, Allah reacted in a similar way to many of my teachers as I presented them with my doubts and questions. Poor Iblis! Elevated to spend time with the Angels only to be told to stay in his lane and then thrown out of heaven for asking a question. My mother has likened me to Iblis many times, and though I would never admit it to her, I don't see it as an insult.

The question of free will versus God's plan really bothered me. While studying Islamic law class, we were learning about the sharia punishment for homosexuals – either being thrown off a tall building or being hanged. I often spent these classes doodling or reading under the desk. This interested me so I had to ask the question which came to me then. Why would God make someone gay and then punish them? Some of my classmates rolled their eyes and others looked at me in anger. The teacher looked at me like I was a small bug stuck to the bottom of her shoe and said that it was an abomination. I said I thought that it was unkind to first make someone gay and then punish them. She looked at me in anger and said Allah never makes anyone commit sin but they do it themselves. I was still perplexed – but if God is all-knowing and knows when we will commit a sin, how could we go against his knowledge of what will happen? She completely lost her patience with me then. She rose to her feet and told me to stand up and say the shahada, the Sunni Islamic declaration of faith:

There is no God but Allah and Muhammad is his final messenger.

I refused. I couldn't see the point that she was trying to make and she had not answered my questions. It all makes sense to me now of course. To have even questioned the execution of gay men under sharia[4] law that she was trying to justify and teach to minors amounted to apostasy in her eyes. She wanted me to say the declaration of faith to prove that I was still Muslim. At the time, I just stood waiting for the punishment, listened to her screaming at me and then took the sticky note to the head teacher's office feeling triumphant because I had successfully convinced one class-mate of my argument before I left the class room.

I feel proud of my younger self, standing up to Islamic homophobia when I was too young to fully appreciate it for what it was. For years I watched institutional homophobia play out as student after student was expelled after being accused of the great crime of lesbianism. We called lesbians 'Lemons' and we knew all about them.

One expulsion haunts me. The girls were only twelve and they were best friends. They were told to pack their bags and wait for their parents to pick them up. People watched them in the corridor as they walked to their bedrooms and muttered 'They're lesbos'. I felt terribly sad for them and I worried about how their parents might handle it. I found one of the affected women years later, and we discussed it briefly. She has pleaded with me to keep her anonymous and said that it was humiliating and that she had not discussed in with anyone else since it had happened. I wondered how it must feel to carry around the burden of that memory so deeply stored away out of shame. She assured me that it was all made up and that she was in fact heterosexual. Whether she was or was not actually doesn't make any difference to me – it is illegal to discriminate on the grounds of sexuality in all schools for a reason.

A part of me mourns always for the teenage girls that were

---

[4] Sharia is Islamic law – please note that there are many schools of Islamic legal thought.

expelled like this and will never get justice. They may never speak up about what happened to them and they may never openly agree with me when I say that whether they were or were not lesbian or bisexual makes no difference, it should never have happened. We did not know our rights and neither did our parents, who also hid what the school did either out of ignorance or societal pressure. Undoubtedly some remained mute in silent complicity.

As I turned 15, I became interested in the local boys who would sit on top of their sheds in adjoining gardens to the school, drinking beer and watching us play rounders on a sunny Sunday afternoon. Once one of the older girls came running on the court, told us all to cover our hair quickly, and shooed the boys away, to my dismay. Our scarves became shorter, our long Islamic dresses became tighter with slits to reveal tight black trousers and we had gathered a reputation amongst Islamic schools for having the most 'tartiest Jamia girls'. I never snuck out of school to meet a boy, but some girls did. Sometimes they would get caught, but mostly not. I wish that those boys were left to watch us play sports; I would have liked to have talked to them.

Part 2: Guarding my chastity

I didn't realise that some people considered me to be beautiful until my twenties. I had been heavily discouraged from trying to look attractive for most of my life. My hijab and jilbab,[5] a long loose dress that came to my feet, were designed to make men not notice me, like an invisibility cloak passed down to me by my mother and passed down to her by distant step-cousins from Saudi Arabia.

[5] Hijab is the head covering by Muslim women and a jilbab is a long loose dress.

Eid was a time of jealousy and resentment during those years. My older sisters were not sent to religious schools because it had not been an option then. Only I truly benefited from the impact of Tony Blair's multicultural Christianity as he broadened the types of religious schools in Britain. My sisters would look so beautiful on Eid in their brightly coloured Pakistani clothes. One Eid, I was left to wear jeans and a t-shirt covered by some ghastly cucumber-coloured jilbab that my Mum had sewn with her own soft hands. I hated it and it was one of the most painful days of my life. Twenty-year-old cousins covered in make-up, hair extensions and perfume would patronise me and say, 'Aw, Mashallah, your hijab makes you look so beautiful; I wish I could find the strength to wear it'.

All I wanted to do then was kick my cousins and set fire to the hijab but it stayed around my head for years. The only moment when it stopped irritating me was at some point during my time in Pakistan. I had begun to believe that I was so ugly with my bushy eyebrows which I wasn't allowed to pluck, no sense of style outside of the Islamic uniform I was put in every day, that there was no point in arguing about the hijab with my mother – what difference would it make?

By 16 I was home from boarding school in disgrace after being publicly expelled for having illegal items like a disposable camera and a book with potty-mouthed gangsters. It might seem strange that I would mourn for my jail after dreaming of escaping for so many years, but I had become used to it. When I was at school I used to press my face against the green metal bars keeping me inside during cold winter mornings and here was my opportunity to be free … so why did I still feel so trapped?

My mum knew that I was still reeling from the shock of the sudden expulsion and she wanted to do something to make me feel better. My sister had studied at the Al-Hudaa institute for women in Pakistan and she had a great experience while she was there.

The school was started by the scholar Dr Farhat Hashmi who spearheads an Islamic fundamentalist and female led evangelising movement in Pakistan. She had set up an institution in Canada and I was asked if I wanted to go there. I felt excited by the prospect of going to Canada and so I quickly jumped at the opportunity.

Women from all over had come here to listen to Hashmi. Her dulcet tones brought joy to my fellow students who wanted to be closer to her and respectfully called her 'Ustatha' – teacher – but she often sent me to sleep (a state I hid by pulling my scarf firmly over my closed eyes). The course in Canada was in Urdu, and, as my proficiency in the language isn't strong, I struggled with it. We learnt that in Pakistan the same course was starting in English at the school in Islamabad so before I knew it, I found myself in the native country of my parents. I had never visited Pakistan before, so a part of me had always been curious to see what it was like. I was happy to be going there. I was the youngest and most educated pupil of Islamic studies in the class, in the one-year Quranic interpretation course. The first thing I noticed about Pakistan were the lack of women in the early hours of the morning as I was in the taxi being taken to my hostel.

The hostel was actually a large room at the back of a house offered up by one of Hashmi's wealthy students. Although she was a nice enough woman, I couldn't help feeling that she resented us being in her home. Even though it was a large room, it was far too small considering that ten women were living there and sleeping on mattresses on the floor. The hostel was for English speaking pupils who had come from Britain, Canada, China and America. It took me a few days to settle in however as someone who had already lived in boarding schools, it wasn't difficult. We had a wonderful cook called Sureya who would tell us stories about her days in a village while we sat in her small kitchen, and who we encouraged to learn to read and write. We had more freedom than the students who stayed at the main hostel for

Pakistani girls. We were allowed mobile phones and we could leave the hostel to go out with friends. I don't know much about the school's main hostel, however I do know through anecdote that it was much stricter than ours. A cheerful driver would pick us up five days a week and take us to class where we would spend six to eight hours a day studying the Quran.

If you pull at the strings of fundamentalist Islam, I believe you will find before you a naked man, shivering from fear of powerful and ordinary women who control their bodies and destinies. Women are often the ones who enforce patriarchal rules on their disobedient daughters, friends, and sisters. It is the gossiping aunties we fear, not their husbands. Our mothers flicker between wanting to let us have the freedoms they didn't have and wanting to keep us protected from the harsh realities of being fallen women.

Over the course of my year in the all-girl's college in Pakistan, I transformed from a rebellious and sceptical teenager to a fully-veiled fundamentalist Muslim who would have justified any kind of sharia execution if you could find me a verse or a 'sound' saying from Muhammad. All the knowledge that I had gained from the Islamic boarding school in Britain finally made sense and I started to believe in it. Day after day, I had nothing to focus on apart from the detailed study of the Quran and the fundamentalist interpretation of it seeped into my mind like poison when I was most vulnerable. I spent nights lamenting the punishments that were going to come upon my liberal and sinful family. How lucky they were that they had me to guide them to the right path!

Part 3: Becoming my own master

Back in England, I started my A levels at the Islamic College of London, where I studied English, Psychology and Sociology. I was deeply religious at this point, praying my five daily prayers and when I could, a sixth prayer in the early hours of the morning. I was teaching children Arabic and Islamic Studies, as well as teaching the interpretation of the Quran in the prayer room of the Islamic College where I was enrolled. No matter how much I prayed or spread the word of Allah, I felt empty. A suffocating depression followed me everywhere I went as I thought-policed myself, and despaired at my own sinfulness.

I wouldn't allow myself to listen to music, digging my nails into my skin out of anxiety if I was stuck somewhere like a shop where music would be playing in the background. I felt disconnected from my sceptical and liberal father who looked at me like I was a stranger in his home. I had stopped wearing the face veil but I kept my long jilbab and hijab on all the time. I think I resented my mother for sending me away and looked down on her for not following my version of fundamentalist Islam.

This was the first time in my life when I had had unfettered access to three sources of information: TV, the internet, and public libraries. Before this, most of the content that I could access was heavily controlled to filter out anything considered too sinful for a good Muslim. At college, I started studying in a way that I was not used to at all. Islam did not enter the classroom, even if some of my teachers were Muslim. I could ask questions and not be laughed at. Instead, my teachers enjoyed my thirst for answers and encouraged me to think critically. I started asking myself the questions I thought I was done with when I embraced fundamentalism in Pakistan. Faith is nothing without trust and some time during my studies abroad, I had put my trust firmly in the Allah of Farhat Hashmi and the Deobandi[6] clerics who had inspired the curriculum at Jamia Al-Hudaa.

[6] The Deobandi tradition is diverse and wide, originating in Deoband, India, in the nineteenth century. It is the most influential form of institutionalised Islam in Britain with an estimated 40 per cent of mosques following its tradition.

The Allah I believed in then was a paradoxical figure: The Most Compassionate as well as one swift to order boiling pus and water to be shoved down the throats of disbelievers and sinners. Unlike some of my Muslim friends and family, hell was not an abstract concept to me. I had spent years reciting, memorising, and studying the detailed verses on the grotesque horrors that awaited disbelievers. Even if I wanted to, I was unable to believe that Allah would not be true to his word. I was convinced that once the Muslims were cleansed of their sins and removed from Hell, the fiery pit still full of kafirs[7] would be sealed forever. I took every word of the Quran to be literal and found the idea that Allah's words could be taken as metaphorical both delusional and arrogant.

During my A level Sociology classes, we took a module on different political perspectives on religion. This was a defining moment during my education at the college because it was the first time that I was really introduced to the concept of feminism. We learnt about different feminist perspectives on religious control, particularly over the bodies of women. For the first time in my life I had found a language that explained my own suffocation at being told to wear this, or do that because I was female. The more I studied feminism, the more my own world started to fall apart. I would lie on my prayer mat, clutching at my hijab like it was a noose, wanting to let my hair run free but also fearing the consequences of divine anger. I toyed with the delicious and frightening idea that I might be able to choose what to do with my own body and life, that perhaps I was free and not a slave to God and family honour.

Questions started coming to me at frightening speed during this time. Why did the Quran sanction the physical abuse of women? If the Quran was the final revelation, why didn't Allah spare a moment to completely ban violence against women? Even

[7] Disbelievers.

52

if many scholars had interpreted the verse to mean hit lightly, with a miswak-like thing, or even that it was only a metaphorical beating, would that not also amount to emotional abuse which is humiliating for women?

I also noticed things that I hadn't before – for instance the Quran hardly speaks directly to women, instead it tends to speak to men about *their* women. I had also started to fall out of love with Muhammad. I was taught that Muhammad married many times and that his favourite wife was only six years old at the time of marriage, and that he slept beside her when she was nine years old. Some Muslim interpretations state that she was 19 years old at the time of their wedding. We were taught that a nine-year-old during the prophet's time was like an adult woman in our age as females matured much faster during that era and we were assured that this was backed up by science. According to the life story of Muhammad that I was taught, he visited her soon before they were betrothed and she was still playing with toys. She had a small winged horse, and he said to her that horses do not fly to which she replied that the prophet Solomon had winged horses. The story that I was taught is that Muhammad realised that he should marry Aisha because of a recurring dream where her picture was shown to him and naturally her father, the prophet's best friend and ally Abu Bakr hastily gave her away to him. Muhammad's marriage to Aisha at the age of six which is supported by narrations of Muhammad considered to be authentic by many scholars is partly the reason it is so difficult to eradicate child marriage in some places such as Saudi Arabia, Pakistan, and Yemen as for some, child marriage is sanctioned because Muhammad's life is taken to be an example for all of mankind.

I don't consider the main sources of the prophet's narrations to be authentic historical sources, but the fact is this, these books are historically sound to many Islamic scholars who hold political power over the lives of millions of people including little girls. The books that were written about Muhammad's life were written many centuries after he died. Imam Bukhari's collection of narrations about Muhammad's lives, the gold standard among many Sunni scholars, say that he travelled through deserts looking for anyone who had heard from someone that someone had heard that someone had heard that Muhammad had said such and such a thing. These narrations attest to whether Muhammad did or didn't marry a child and in my view the methods used by scholars of hadith are not rigorous enough for us to actually know whether it happened or not. What is more alarming is that many scholars are willing to justify and accept these narrations irrespective of the impact it has on child marriage laws in some parts of the world.

Aisha was my favourite of the prophet's wives. She was fiery, intelligent, jealous, and waged war against Ali, the nephew and son-in-law of Muhammad after he died according to the legend. I have read many Muslim feminists hold up Khadija, Muhammad's first wife, as proof that Islam is not a sexist, out-of-date religion. After all it was she who propositioned him and she was richer and much older than Muhammad. However, what many fail to mention is that the same sources that give them their accounts of Khadija to soothe the minds of Western liberals, support the idea that Aisha was only a child when he married her. I have noticed that Islamic feminists skirt over Aisha's story, perhaps feeling too uncomfortable to discuss the claims that Muhammad had a sexual relationship with a child.

To this day, I feel more secure criticising the idea of God, than to speak against Muhammad. My mother always warns me – say what you will of God but don't criticise Muhammad otherwise the mob will find you. She is right to give me this advice. Look to some of the most prominent cases of blasphemy in the world, and you will see that judges and civilians rush to condemn people who dare to criticise the final prophet. Every so often I think of Christian woman Asia Bibi, who is rotting away on death row in Pakistan because some village women said that she criticised Muhammad, a claim that she vehemently denies. A living and breathing woman is still locked away from her children and denied her freedom because she was accused of tarnishing a dead man's name.

I started visiting churches and cathedrals when my doubts really weighed on me, to people-watch other worshippers. I spent many hours in Southwark Cathedral, listening to the choir boys singing beautifully, wondering whether I was doomed and going to burn alongside them. Christianity did not tempt me I didn't bother to study it deeply as I thought Islam was the most superior religion. I had been taught that all religions, including Buddhism, start off as Islam, and then they get corrupted as time passes. When Muslims read the first chapter of the Quran during their daily prayers, they ask God not to make them like the people who were led astray nor like those who had make God angry. We believed that the first group were the Christians who blasphemously attributed a son to God and the second group are Jews who feature repeatedly in the Quran for some misdeed or another.

The internet became my friend as I spent a long time searching for arguments against Islam, desperate for it to not be true. Some of you reading this might think that my heart wasn't pure at the time, and therefore the devil was able to completely take over. It is true that I wanted someone to convince me that it wasn't true so that I could let go of the terror that took over me whenever I thought billions of people burning in hell, their skins healed and burned all over again. I wanted to be told that I didn't have to wear hijab and that I wasn't immodest for it. I wanted to listen to music and dance like the women I saw on TV, I wanted to be a freer version of myself. Yes, I wanted to throw away the chains that were placed on me to make me into a good woman ready to serve her husband and children. My belief in Islam started to ebb slowly away as I understood the theory of evolution and watched video after video of atheists debating prominent Muslim scholars. Christopher Hitchens and Richard Dawkins, although I accept that they aren't perfect prophets, were some of my earliest atheistic influences.

I was both shocked and amused by their candid criticism of Muhammad and the claim that the Quran was a peaceful book which contained the perfectly conserved word of God. I allowed the doubt to take root inside me and stopped fighting it. I could read the Quran critically and some of the fear that I felt when I read verses about disbelievers left me. I was no longer able to justify the punishments for disbelievers or punishments such as cutting off a thief's hand. I pushed aside the scholarly footnotes that preached caution before carrying out any of the Quran's violent punishments and couldn't help but see it as nothing more than a man-made thing like the Talmud or the Bible if it needed so many words of human caution to stop people carrying out acts of violence masked as God's divine order.

There was a defining moment for me when any belief I had left in God was wiped out from me completely. I was listening to Carl Sagan reading from his book *The Pale Blue Dot*. He spoke about an image and when I googled it I was shocked. It was an image of a tiny blue dot, suspended in a beam of light – earth. I was so consumed at that point with the idea of a very rigid concept of God and Islam. When I truly realised how tiny the earth is in comparison to the rest of the universe, I couldn't believe in a tiny God who was waiting to line human beings up after punishing some of them in the grave, to ask them why they didn't wear hijab or why they didn't believe in him. I felt a peace the like of which I haven't experienced again, a reassuring conviction that this was my only life and that I won't have the suffer the torment of being tortured in hell or knowing that others were being tortured for eternity. Some former Muslims say that doubting caused them great anxiety and fear, but for me it was exhilarating. I felt like I could breathe again when I realised that it was possible that Islam simply was a religion like any other whose outlook on the world could be inaccurate.

The first thing I did after this was to remove my hijab. I thought about it for days and I had decided that I was going to finally do it. I left my home on an ordinary day, turned the street corner, placed my fingers around the pin that fastened the cloth around my hair and I pulled. It felt incredible and I peered into a car window to see the reflection of the person that I wanted to be – the Aliyah who was hidden inside. The removal of my hijab sent shockwaves through my family who felt that something was seriously wrong. They quickly found out that I no longer believed in Islam and they were devastated. My relationship with my parents and most of my siblings broke down after this for a few years. We stayed in touch but my lack of belief was always the elephant in the room. I felt unwanted and unloved now that they knew who I really was. They begged me not to tell anyone else that I didn't believe in Islam and I pretended to be a Muslim at family gatherings and online for the best part of 6 years. I lost many friends during this time which caused a great amount of sadness but it also taught me a valuable lesson. When love is conditional and judgement takes its place, it is no longer a love worth holding on to. The one person who was confused and conflicted but held on to me for dear life was my mother. She is a complicated and wonderful woman – the Queen of my life. She took it badly, not understanding how I could abandon Islam and without meaning to we have both hurt one another, but we have managed to hold on to each other. Our relationship is better now than it has ever been as she has accepted who I am and she understands that I am still the daughter she always loved.

I am grateful that I now have close relationships with all of my immediate family and my mother made sure that nobody in my extended family could say anything to me; she stood between me and judgemental eyes at family weddings like a lioness protecting her cubs. Not all former Muslims can rebuild the relationships that break down as ordinary people get caught in the cross fire between tradition, taboo, and the instinct to protect and nurture their children. Sometimes parents go too far, say, or do things that strike too deeply at their children's sense of dignity and self-respect.

After years of keeping my beliefs to myself and close friends, I was given an opportunity to break the silence. I was given a platform to speak about my experiences at the Islamic boarding school in Britain by well-known ex-Muslim activist Maryam Namazie. The discussion of the Trojan scandal had broken in the news and I was angry that people were only outraged about the practices that went on in my school every day because it involved taxpayers' money.[1] The video of my speech went online and it didn't take long for members of my extended family to find out. My mother was floored when she started receiving calls from people in Pakistan, Birmingham, and Walsall to ask how I could be calling myself an atheist. My father sent a message to the family through my mother, 'If you want to speak about it to me then get in touch but I don't want your opinion'. Unsurprisingly hardly anyone called him but my mother took on most of the people calling. She defended me and said that she had to keep me close to her now that I had gone public because she felt I was in danger. I wept when I heard that women were making fun of her and I felt guilty. I also knew that it wasn't my fault that these women were being cruel and that I am not responsible for their

[1] The Trojan Horse Scandal was the outcome of an anonymous letter sent to a city council in Birmingham with the allegation that Islamists were infiltrating state schools in Muslim-heavy areas.

actions. I couldn't bear being silent anymore, it devastated me when I met teenagers who were depressed and suicidal because they felt like outsiders. I had started meeting ex-Muslims and I realised that I wasn't the only one who felt isolated and ashamed. It dawned on me that there is a real prejudice against people who leave Islam and that it was systematic as well as wide spread.

I am humble enough to acknowledge that I do not have all the answers; however, I have learnt that oppressed people must stand up, make themselves known, be proud to break down any kind of prejudice. When it comes to oppressed groups, often it is not what is being said that counts, but that it was said at all. How could I expect my counterparts in Pakistan, Saudi Arabia, and Iran to do it if I didn't have the courage to do it here in the United Kingdom, one of the safest places in the world to be an atheist? I went on to found Faith to Faithless with Imtiaz Shams and we have managed to raise awareness in media outlets across the world, and our organisation has joined forces with the largest non-religious charity in Britain, Humanists UK.

We work with apostates, people who have left religions and cults, from all backgrounds, not only people who have left Islam. This experience has taught me that the discrimination which affects ex-Muslims also affects people from other groups such as in the case of former Jehovah's Witnesses who can face excommunication and shunning. Last year I visited Plymouth Humanists and a woman cried during my talk. I spoke to her later and she had left a Christian denomination and had lost her family and friends because of it. She spoke about how lonely she has felt and that she was glad to have met someone who understood what she was dealing with.

I believe that the prejudice affecting apostates is a social issue that can be resolved through social change, awareness, and theological reform. If the loved ones of apostates understood what it felt like for us, appreciated that we have the right to our beliefs, and understood that we need support, then maybe many relationships and even lives could be saved. There are people out there who have suffered violence and whose mental health has been adversely affected just because they no longer believe in a religion. Some of these people can find support networks; unfortunately there are and will be people who will slip through the cracks and they will feel that there is no escape for them. I have been suicidal in the past when I planned to take my own life because there were dark moments when I felt like I couldn't bear the pain of feeling so alone and unlovable any longer. I am grateful to the people and organisations who saved my life and I am glad that I am here writing this today.

The years of fundamentalism have shaped me, but they do not define who I am any longer. I forget how things used to be but every so often I am vividly reminded of the simple freedoms that I have fought for. I could be standing in a nightclub, surrounded by friends, a cocktail in my hand or swimming in a bikini in a warm sea and I will be suddenly reminded of how things used to be. I have come out on the other side, stronger and bolder. If I could go back and speak to my younger self, I would comfort and hold her, try to reassure her that she won't always feel like this. It is difficult to convince people who are in despair that things can get better, but they really can. My final words of advice to anyone who is going through what I have been through are: you are enough, don't stay isolated, reach out; you do not have to feel ashamed and you deserve to be treated with love and respect.

LOSING FAITH AT FIFTY

HASSAN RADWAN

My earliest memory was reciting al-Fatiha, the short first chapter of the Quran, at bedtime. It made me feel God was watching over me and cared. My father, or more usually, my mother, would stand at the door, while my two brothers and I folded our arms. We recited it by heart at lightning speed in Arabic and English, then heads down, lights out. Sometimes I also added my own special prayer quietly to myself: 'Please God, make everything all right'. I was too tired to go through the details. I was certain God understood. My father, Aziz Radwan, was a headmaster and a strict disciplinarian. Born to a wealthy Muslim Egyptian family in Cairo, he was full of paradoxes. In some ways he was ultra-conservative yet in other ways he could be very liberal-minded. He brought us up as Muslims but never tried to force anything on us. He used to say, 'Religion is about how you treat people.' At one point he sent me to a Sunday School for Egyptian expat children, but I hated it so much he took me out. He did bring a Tunisian Sheikh to teach us Arabic & Quran at home but I think we teased the poor sheikh so much he gave up. My mother, Mary Magson, was the daughter of Horace Magson, an accountant from Darlington. Her family were Methodists, but she converted to Islam largely to please my father (who in turn wanted to please his father). She always used to say, 'It's all the same God.' Neither were religious in an orthodox way yet believed in God and taught us that religion was about good behaviour and good character.

Throughout my childhood I was not very religious, and often resented the fact I had been given this funny name and exotic religion in a country where few shared them at that time. But as I reached my late teens, a series of events caused me to re-think my views. The first was the Islamic Revolution in Iran. I remember watching the television coverage of running battles on the streets of Tehran, between the ordinary people and the heavily armed guard of the Shah. I found the images inspiring: defiant civilians rising up against the might of a tyrant. My rebellious spirit saw it as a people's struggle against a brutal dictator, but I was also aware the role religion was playing – my religion, Islam.

I was confronted with another example of the power of religion when my close friend returned from a camping trip to announce he was now a born-again Christian. He became irritatingly exultant about his faith and constantly attempted to convert me. But the more my friend explained things such as the Trinity, Original Sin and Atonement, the more I knew these were concepts I could never believe in. The idea that God is 'Three persons in One' and that man is born sinful because of the sin of another, or that sins are not forgiven because of any meritorious act by the person themselves, but because someone else was sacrificed for them, all conflicted with my sense of justice and reason.

Around this time, I had gone camping with friends to the Deeply Vale music festival in Lancashire. As we walked up one side of the valley and looked down at the campfires and tents I heard a sound I never expected to hear. It was the Arabic call to prayer. It resonated with a strange clarity above the hubbub of the festival below. I couldn't understand why someone was reciting the Muslim call to prayer at a music festival and I began to feel that perhaps it was my own personal wake-up call to faith.

A few months later I saw Cat Stevens on television, giving a farewell concert. He had become a Muslim, changed his name to Yusuf Islam and was resigning from the music business, turning his back on fame and fortune to devote his life to his new-found faith. The public were mystified. Why would someone who had it all want to throw it away for religion? But I felt inspired and proud. If such a creative and respected person saw something worthwhile in Islam, perhaps I, as someone born with an Islamic heritage, should take it more seriously?

The final episode in this series of events was when my father turned up unexpectedly to invite me to go with him to Egypt for a couple of weeks. I was now 19 years old and at a crossroads in my life. Unsure of my identity and where I was going, I thought a two-week holiday would be a pleasant distraction. The moment I stepped off the plane and into the hot, moist atmosphere of Cairo airport, I felt I was in another universe. The scent of incense drifted through an intricate lattice window. Donkeys laden with vegetables weaved their way through an orchestra of blaring car horns; street merchants announced their wares with a siren cry that made me jump; men wearing pyjamas prayed on the pavement; women threw buckets of peelings from balconies above. It was a mad, chaotic patchwork quilt of smells, noise and colour and came as quite a culture shock. But, despite its strangeness, I soon felt very at home. For the first time I didn't have to hide or be embarrassed about my origins. Moreover, everyone admired and respected both halves of my cultural background, the English as well as the Egyptian.

We stayed at my Uncle Fouad's house in Cairo – he was a civil servant in the Ministry of Health. Egyptians wore western clothes, watched dubbed Hollywood movies, and had many of the modern conveniences found in England. But as I sat on the replica eighteenth-century French furniture in the ornate lounge surrounded by framed prints of Vermeer's *The Lacemaker* and Da Vinci's *Mona Lisa*, a loudspeaker in the street outside began bellowing the call to prayer. This triggered a wave of prayer calls that slowly unfurled across the Cairo rooftops and off into the distance. Even on television, Clark Gable was cut off in mid flow, as a sign came up in Arabic, announcing the evening prayer. When everyone got up to pray, I was left sitting alone at the table. I felt a little uncomfortable.

After prayer my cousin Nihal showed me a picture in a newspaper of Ayatollah Khomeini hugging a little girl. 'Aww, he is such a good man!' she said. 'He says there is no difference between Sunni and Shi'ah. He says we are all Muslims and should be united.' Nihal was a very strong-minded, independent young woman, who took her freedom to do as she pleased for granted. She didn't wear a headscarf and had very western habits and tastes. Yet she seemed completely comfortable identifying with very orthodox Islamic views – views with which most Egyptians I met seemed totally at ease, despite appearing to be relatively westernised.

'Eat, Hassan!' said Auntie Ola as she sat next to me. 'We made you English food: fish and chips!'

'Do you say your prayers, Hassan?' asked Uncle Fouad.

'To be honest, no, I don't.'

'Oh, you must pray! Prophet Muhammad said: "Prayer is the key to Paradise".'

'Why does God need us to pray?'

'God doesn't need us to pray. But we need to pray. To give thanks and seek his help.'

Uncle Fouad took a Quran from the shelf.

'Have you read the Quran, Hassan?'

'A bit.'

He passed it to me: 'I want you to promise me you will read it.'

I was reluctant to promise something I didn't want to do, but as I was a guest in his house I could hardly refuse. I thought I could read a few pages then politely put it to one side.

'Thanks. Okay, I will.'

'Insha-Allah,' prompted Uncle Fouad.

'Insha-Allah,' I replied.

The next day my father and Uncle Fouad went out, leaving me at home with Auntie Ola. So, I picked up the Quran, as promised, and began to read. To my surprise I found I couldn't put it down. The Quran is not like any ordinary book. It doesn't follow any of the conventions of standard prose. It has no definite beginning nor end. There is no plot to follow and no neat resolution. It jumps abruptly from one account to another. Even its style changes with little warning, from a steady narrative to fast paced rhyming prose. Yet I found it strangely irresistible.

'Alif Lam Mim.'

I looked up at Auntie Ola; 'What does Alif Lam Mim mean?'

'Nobody knows.' She smiled. 'Some chapters of the Quran begin with letters of the alphabet. Scholars have tried to explain them. But nobody knows for sure.'

'You mean it's a mystery?'

'Yes.'

I liked mysteries.

'God is the Light of the heavens and the earth. The Parable of His Light is as if there were a Niche and within it a Lamp: the Lamp enclosed in Glass: the glass like a brilliant star: Lit from a blessed Tree, an Olive, neither of the East nor of the West, whose oil is well-nigh luminous, though fire scarce touched it: Light upon Light!' (24:35)

'When my servants ask you about me, (say) I am indeed close and answer the prayer of the one who calls on me.' (2:186)

'Wherever you turn your face, there is God's presence. God is all-Pervading.' (2:115)

'Do not turn away from men with pride, nor walk arrogantly through the earth, but be moderate in your pace and lower your voice.' (31:18)

'Treat with kindness your parents and kindred, and orphans and those in need; speak fair to the people; be steadfast in prayer; and practice regular charity.' (2:83)

'We made you into nations and tribes so that you may get to know one another. Indeed, the best among you in the sight of God, is the best in conduct.' (49:13)

I began to cry. I felt silly and I tried to hide my tears from Auntie Ola. But I couldn't stop. I felt a strange force deep within. I was certain it was the gentle and loving presence of God. It was as though a veil had been lifted and I had discovered the meaning and identity I'd been searching for since I was a child. It was a deeply spiritual and emotional time for me. I spent most of the two weeks reading the Quran and meeting members of my extended family. There, also, the conversations invariably turned to religion.

'A friend of mine says Jesus died for our sins.'

'The Quran says the opposite,' said Magdi: 'No soul shall bear the burden of another.' (17:15)

Magdi gave me a book of hadith which I read from cover to cover. One hadith in particular touched me deeply and remains amongst my favourites:

'(God says) I am as my servant thinks of me. I am with him when he remembers me. If he comes to me a hand's span; I come to him an arm's length. If he comes to me one arm's length, I draw near to him by two outstretched arms. If he comes to me walking, I come to him running.' (Bukhari, 16:1435)

When it came time to return to England I didn't want to leave, and vowed I'd be back soon. It had been an amazing experience and I felt a sense of intrepid excitement, as though a magical door had been opened. I came back to England full of zeal and determination to immerse myself in the practice and study of my faith.

The awakening of my own faith seemed to coincide with a general Islamic awakening in the UK during the late 1970s and early 1980s. I don't know whether this rise in Islamic awareness was prompted by world events at the time, but many second-generation Muslims in the UK were beginning to re-discover the religion of their birth, after a long period of having been Muslim only in name. There was an air of excitement and dynamism about the Muslim community, particularly in London. Study circles and informal gatherings sprang up in living rooms or community centres. Each Friday, the display window in the foyer of Regent's Park Mosque seemed to be more and more packed with little cards announcing new events. Even greeting someone with Salaams after prayers prompted an invitation to a Zikr (Remembrance of Allah) or a Halaqa (Islamic Discussion Circle).

When I took part in such meetings I was struck by the diversity of those attending: Asians, Europeans, Africans, Turks, Kurds, Arabs, Malaysians and Iranians – you name it. They came from all walks of life: civil servants, students, bus drivers, doctors and parking attendants. There was no barrier of race, class or nationality. Being a Muslim was the only thing that mattered and it granted instant membership of the Ummah (community). The aim of the Islamic meetings was to learn about Islam, but equally important was the social side – getting to know other Muslims in the area and building up a sense of brotherhood. I enrolled for a degree in Arabic and Islamic Studies at the School of Oriental and African Studies (SOAS). My tutor was David Cowan, the author of *Modern Literary Arabic*, an elderly but sprightly Scotsman who converted to Islam in his youth. As a young Muslim keen to soak up everything I could about Islam, I found the atmosphere at SOAS invigorating, and I attended every extra-curricular lecture and debate. I devoured anything and everything that had Islam as its subject matter, and the SOAS Library became my home. I stayed there studying until late into the night and regularly had to be asked to leave by staff locking up.

In between my own efforts to learn more about Islam, I was also busy spreading the word to others. I was motivated by an ardent desire to share what I had discovered and to save them from hellfire. A friend invited me to join him on a 'Tablighi Jamaat', a movement aimed at bringing Muslims back to the path of pure Islam. I found myself on a long road trip heading to the Dewsbury Mosque nestled in the Yorkshire moors. There we listened to talks and invited locals to come and pray and listen to lectures. The experience of being isolated in the mosque for two weeks – cut off from the world around – had a profound effect on me. By the time I returned home I found my priorities had shifted. I was less concerned about this life and far more focused on the next life. I grew my beard, wore a white jilbab and cap. I not only prayed all the compulsory prayers, but I prayed all the extra prayers, too. I did my best to follow each and every Sunnah [2] I could. I began fasting every Monday; I would sip water in three breath pauses; enter a door with my right foot; sleep on my right side; use a miswak daily for my teeth, and so on. I was determined to keep in my mind that heightened state of fear of God that I had felt at the Dewsbury Mosque. I was president of the SOAS Students' Union Islamic

[2] The sunnah is everything related to the life, deeds and sayings of the prophet Muhammad. Here, it refers to additional prayers that Muslims read during the five daily prayers which the prophet Muhammad was said to have read.

Society from 1981 until 1984. During my presidency I set up an Islamic bookstall, organised talks, debates, films, a prayer room and permission to use one of the lecture rooms for Friday Prayers. We shared the responsibility of giving the Khutbah[3] among ourselves as well as inviting speakers from outside such as Adil Salahi, the translator of Sayyid Qutb's tafseer *In the Shade of the Qur'an* and Dr Kalim Siddiqui, the Director of The Muslim Institute in Endsleigh Street, and his understudy, Dr Ghayasuddin.

I also used to attend sermons by the well-known Sufi, Sheikh Nazim. I greatly admired the writings and poetry of some of the great Sufi luminaries like Ibn Arabi and Rumi. But I was a little disappointed with what I had witnessed at Sheikh Nazim's circles. Not so much with Sheikh Nazim himself, who was a very warm and charismatic speaker, but by the way his followers fawned upon him. It seemed to be somewhat cultish and clashed with my idea of Sufism being about conquering the ego. It had been my spiritual search for meaning and identity that had brought me to Islam. I was attracted by the mystical passages of the Quran and the promise of inner knowledge and enlightenment. But once I became a practising Muslim it was taken for granted that I would support the political stance of other Muslims on issues such as Palestine, Kashmir, Afghanistan, and, later on, on Bosnia, Chechnya and Iraq. There was certainly a lot going on at the time and Muslims were rarely off the TV screens, from the assassination of Egypt's President Anwar el-Sadat by a group called Islamic Jihad – amongst its members was Ayman Zawahiri – to the Iran Hostage Crisis and bombing of the US embassy in Beirut.

Traditional views of Islam see no division between politics and religion. There is no 'Render unto Caesar the things that

[3] Khutbah refers to the sermon which is given after Friday prayers.

are Caesar's and unto God the things that are God's'. Prophet Muhammad was a military and political leader as well as a spiritual leader and applied Islam to every part of life, both the public and the private. Muslims were to be regarded as one body; 'If one part of the body feels pain, then the whole body suffers.' Therefore, I felt my commitment to Islam meant a commitment to my Muslim brothers and sisters around the world. I began to take a keen interest in global politics and read about conflicts and countries I had previously known nothing about. The major issues at the time were the Iranian Islamic revolution, the Russian invasion of Afghanistan and of course the ongoing issue of Palestinians.

The plight of the Palestinians was highlighted in 1982 when unarmed Palestinian men women and children in the Sabra and Shatila refugee camps, were massacred by Christian militia while the camps were surrounded by the Israeli military. I remember seeing pictures of whole families lying dead in the narrow streets, their bodies bloated by the hot sun, hands still clutching the ID papers they had been desperately showing. The images created enormous anger within me. I also felt huge frustration that Muslim leaders were doing nothing to help. The Russian invasion of Afghanistan triggered quite different emotions. The struggle of the Mujahideen against the might of a superpower was inspiring and it seemed to confirm the oft-repeated claim that only by returning to 'pure Islam' could Muslims ever put right injustices we had suffered.

Despite this, most Islamic meetings in the early 1980s were broad-minded and inclusive to begin with. The East Finchley Da'wa Society, of which I became the Amir along with my brother, was a typical example. It was a meeting specifically for young Muslims who wanted to learn more about the faith of their birth. The meetings were mixed and informal and we rotated the leadership amongst the members on a weekly basis. A diverse group of speakers was invited, including Sheikh Darsh from Regent's Park Mosque, a delegation from The Federation of Student Islamic Societies, the modernist Dr Essawi, and Brother Yusuf Islam. The Da'wa society produced its own magazine called *The Clarion,* which I edited, and it included articles about Islam and topical issues. We also organised sports activities, camping trips and excursions. But by the mid-1980s the Da'wa Society had already begun to change. The hard-line and narrow-minded political Islamic groups began creeping into meetings. I was never attracted by such militant groups. I was deeply religious and some often confuse 'religious' with 'extremist', but this is simply not true. Most of us at the Da'wa Society were religious and spiritual, but not interested in political forms of Islam.

The most prominent of these militant groups were the Salafis – also known as Wahhabis – who espoused a literalist and puritanical form of Islam that seeks to cleanse the religion of what they regard as innovations, superstitions and heresies. Throughout the 1980s, Saudi Arabia financed the spread of Salafi doctrine and subsidised Salafi books flooded Muslim bookshops up and down the country. They also set up offices such as the Muslim World League, in Tottenham Court Road, that gave financial help to Islamic organisations, mosques, schools, students and individuals who were willing to adopt their views. Since Muslims had no other source to turn to when they needed help, most, if not all, were willing to accept the strings attached, thinking it was not a serious problem. I myself applied to the Muslim World League for a grant to study Arabic and Islam in Egypt. I was offered a place – not in Egypt, where they considered the teaching to be deviant, but at Medina University in Saudi Arabia. There the curriculum was carefully prepared and taught by Salafi teachers, to ensure that all the students would learn 'true' Islam. Fortunately, by the time I had to make my decision, I had been offered a place at SOAS and so was able to turn it down, but my brother decided to take up a similar offer and left the UK to study at Medina University.

The Salafis were not the only group gaining ground at the time. Hizbu-Tahrir (literally, the Party of Liberation) were their main competitor for the hearts and minds of young British Muslims. One of their prominent members at the time, Farid Kasim, became a regular visitor to our Da'wa Society meetings. His one overriding obsession was the 'Islamic State' (Khilafah). He listened to our talks, not to learn or contribute, but to hijack them and talk about the Khilafah. Farid and his mentor Omar Bakri were too radical even for Hizbu-Tahrir, and they left to form an even more militant group called Al-Muhajiroun.

Islam places great emphasis on marriage and as a young single Muslim I was soon being encouraged to get married 'to complete my Deen' and so in 1983 I was introduced to a devout Muslimah and we married a short while later that year. As those who are married with children know it can have the effect of bringing you down to earth and focus you on the more mundane mechanics of worldly matters. It can also have the effect of cementing your beliefs and lifestyle as they are now shared with your partner. Your investment in them becomes almost set in stone as you bring up your children according to those beliefs and lifestyles. I had five children in total across two marriages (not at the same time I hasten to add); my baby daughter Huda was premature and died in hospital a week after she was born. I remember staying up every night praying and making Du'a to God to save her and make her well. When she died I consoled myself with God knows best; it was a test; it was for the best; she is in a better place. I also blamed myself. I must have failed somewhere at being a good Muslim. I tried even harder to be better Muslim.

After graduating and working briefly in the civil service I completed a Postgraduate Certificate of Education and began my thirty years as a school teacher – fifteen of those years I spent as a senior teacher at Islamia School – the one founded by Yusuf Islam. Islamia School was both a mad and a wonderful place. The sincerity, commitment and genuine warmth of the individuals involved made me feel part of a huge family, albeit a rather odd and dysfunctional family. Throughout my years there it was always much more than a job. I mixed socially with the teachers and parents: we attended prayers together; went to the same Islamic circles; my children played with their children. Even though now I no longer support the idea of religious schools I have to admit that my years there were amongst the happiest years of my life.

I first met Yusuf Islam in 1980 when I attended a circle called 'The Companions of the Mosque' which he led in Regent's Park Mosque, but I got to know him well during the years I spent as a teacher at Islamia School. He had founded the school in 1983 with a small group of parents – my sister and her husband amongst them. They wanted to provide an Islamic alternative to the secular schools. To some it meant importing traditional systems of rote learning and corporal punishment they had been used to in their country of origin. To others born and educated in the UK it meant adopting the methods and curriculum of the West, with minor 'Islamic' concessions. My own commitment to the cause of Islamia School was related to the crisis of identity that I had experienced as a child. I hoped the school would give Muslim children in the UK a strong sense of their identity as British Muslims. I wanted them to feel confident about who they were and have others around them who shared their values and beliefs. Yusuf Islam, who became the chair of the board of governors, had a holistic vision of Islamic education as it had existed during the golden age of Islamic history and wanted a school that could combine the spiritual with the temporal.

Islamia School changed and evolved over the years as it struggled to find its identity. At first it adopted many of the strict

Salafi views – partly because the school relied on donations from wealthy Saudis. The School's Trust Office who raised donations were strongly influenced by Salafi doctrines and relations between them and the more liberal-minded teachers were often very strained. The Trust Office appointed an 'Islamisation Officer' – a parent who had studied in Saudi Arabia, to check school books for 'un-Islamic' content. I was English co-ordinator at the time and was told to provide him with the school's text books. He was given a small office and a little stamp that that read 'Un-Islamic Content'. He would flick through the books and when he saw something he didn't like, down came the stamp in the middle of the page. Even some of our cleaners were telling us what to do. I arrived at school one morning to find someone had written a Hadith of the Prophet, across our class display of Ancient Egypt: 'Whoever makes a picture will be punished on the Day of Judgment and will be asked to give life to what he has created!'

On other occasions faces were blotted out or displays torn. All this would happen during the evening when no one was around. One morning we had a visit from the then Secretary of State for Education, John Patten. As I took him down the corridor I saw, to my horror, that the 'Night Patrol' had been busy censoring an alphabet strip up ahead. Someone had carefully painted correction fluid over all the faces. I looked the other way and pretended not to notice. I don't know if John Patten did the same, but nothing was said.

Sadly, this type of self-appointed moral busybody has long been the bane of Muslim communities. They take their cue from the verse: 'You order what is right and forbid evil.' As a result, they feel they have a divine duty to act as moral police, poking their noses into other people's affairs. It is not uncommon to be approached by complete strangers who without so much as simple greeting start telling you what you are doing is wrong and how to live your life. I remember cheerfully greeting a young Algerian cleaner with salaams and a playful salute as I arrived at school one morning. He frowned and told me saluting was not part of Islam.

The balance of power at Islamia School shifted when Sheikh Ahmad Babakir was appointed as the School's Imam. He came from a very inclusive Sufi tradition and was a staunch opponent of the literalist Salafi teachings. Sheikh Ahmad became extremely popular with the children and teachers alike. He was a warm and immediately likeable personality, who related to children well. He was able to communicate at their level and used jokes and funny voices to make them laugh as he recounted stories and wisdoms to them. Both the adults and the children eagerly looked forward to his assemblies. He had a deep and encyclopaedic knowledge of Islam which he was able to relate to everyday matters. There was always a queue of children and adults outside his door waiting to consult him. Yusuf too was greatly impressed with Sheikh Ahmad and put his support behind him. The final blow to the Salafi influence at Islamia School came when state funding was granted by Tony Blair's New Labour Government in 1998. The school no longer had to dance to the tune of outside donors.

I was teaching in class on 11 September 2001, as the news of the World Trade Center attacks began filtering through. I remember there was an eerie silence as I drove home after school. I switched the TV on as soon as I got in and I think I sat there the whole evening, just watching the planes crash into the World Trade Centre over and over again. I asked myself how could anyone do such a thing in the name of God and my religion. My first instinct was to distance my religion from such an atrocity. These people must have been motivated by a twisted sense of grievance be it political, social or psychological. But I couldn't escape the thought that my religion also played a part. I knew that Islam can lend itself to violent interpretations. I knew such interpretations can strip otherwise sane human beings of their humanity, replacing reason and common sense with a robotic slavery to a very harsh literalist reading of the texts. I began to reflect on my search for meaning and truth, how I had felt when I first became a practising Muslim as a teenager, on the threshold of a higher understanding of God and spiritual enlightenment. I realised that somewhere along the way I had been led astray. Obsessed by form and ritual, worried whether my soap contained pig fat or the food I just bought contained E numbers. Without noticing, I had been diverted, inch by inch. The very things that had led me to Islam, my heart and mind, now seemed to be locked away in a little box, as though I was afraid of them, afraid to think for myself, afraid to step outside a life of imitation and conformity to a set of rules that I hoped would bring me salvation. I asked myself: was slavish submission truly God's ultimate concern for mankind? Was entry to heaven simply a mechanical process that did not involve the heart and mind, but only blind obedience – as the Quran says, 'We hear and we obey.'

Little by little doubts began creeping in. At first, I tried to suppress them and reacted to criticism of Islam with denial, anger and blame. I denied there was anything wrong, felt hypersensitive to criticism and blamed the West for provoking and creating problems. But I couldn't help looking at the Quran in a much more critical way – something we Muslims never truly do. Our starting point is that it is the perfect word of God and reading it is an act of devotion not critical assessment. Any problems that are highlighted are due to our flawed and limited understanding and any energy spent dwelling on them is only directed at absolving the Quran rather than entertaining the slightest possibility it could be wrong. However, I was determined to be brutally honest with myself and began to asking painful questions. Amongst the verses that troubled me, the following stood out, as it was difficult to dismiss using the usual 'context' argument.

'As for those women from whom you fear rebellion (first) admonish them (next), refuse to share their beds, (and last) hit them.' (4:34)

I tried many times to explain it in a way that made sense, but it gnawed at my conscience. This was brought much more into focus by real-life instances of domestic abuse that I heard about. Of course, I knew domestic abuse was an evil that exists in all cultures and all societies, but giving divine sanction for a man to hit his wife – no matter how light and restricted – surely doesn't help matters. I read books and articles about the subject and spoke to as many Sheikhs as I could. They repeated the arguments I had heard many times that the conditions and restrictions which the Quran placed upon wife beating amounted to a virtual ban, particularly since Muslims are obligated to follow the Prophet's example and he never laid a finger on his wives, saying 'The best of you is the best to his wife.' The prophet also said such hitting must be 'not severe' (ghayr mubarrih) and so the scholars say it must be 'light' and was just a symbolic show of displeasure to be administered using a feather, handkerchief or a miswak (tooth stick). I couldn't help thinking that if it was true that these restrictions amount to a ban, then why not just ban it? The Quran had no problem banning polytheism which was far more entrenched religiously and financially (and didn't hurt anyone).

Online I came across interpretations that claimed the words 'hit them' (wadriboohunna) really means 'leave them alone!' – or even 'Make love to them!' I had studied classical Arabic all my life and I knew that these explanations were simply ridiculous. Desperate attempts to deny reality. The word hit (daraba in Arabic) means 'hit'. It can be used metaphorically, but only when used with a preposition (from/about/in etc) and/or an adverb like 'example' (mathalan). Plus, it's inconceivable that all-wise and all-knowing God would use the word 'hit' as a metaphor in a passage where the *last* thing they want is to give the impression it means 'hit'. As for hitting your wife with a feather, handkerchief or miswak, this is simply an insult to human intelligence and dignity.

I tried to convince myself it was my instincts that were wrong and I should just submit to the divine word, without trying to apply my own defective reasoning to it. God cannot be wrong? I must be wrong! I should simply accept that God knows that which I do not. I should hold fast to the 'rope of Allah'. But the doubts persisted and once I doubted one verse I soon found myself doubting others, particularly those about Jahannam:

'As often as their skins are roasted off We shall exchange them for fresh skins' (4:56)

'Boiling fluid will be poured down onto their heads; it will melt their stomachs and skins. For them will be hooked rods of iron Whenever, in their anguish, they try to escape from Hell, they shall be dragged back ...' (22:19-23)

'scorching water like melted brass, that will melt their faces' (18:28-30)

'Like molten brass it will boil in their intestines. Like the scalding of searing water. (It will be said) "Seize him and drag him into the midst of the Blazing Fire! Then pour over his head the torment of scorching Water"' (44:43-48)

'Dragged through scalding fetid fluid and burnt in the Fire' (40: 70-72)

'No food except pus' (69:36)

'They will be given boiling water to drink so that it tears their bowels to pieces' (47:15)

'Never will it be eased off them nor will they be given respite' (3:88)

'Never will they get out' (5:37)

'Hell for all eternity' (4:169)

Hell had never made sense to me and was one of those issues I placed in a box labelled: 'God will explain later' and placed high up on the shelf out of sight. But now I could no longer avoid examining it. How can it make any sense for God to torture his flawed creation without end? The torments of Hell are described in the most gruesome and graphic detail in over 500 places throughout the Quran. They detail how God will keep unbelievers alive replacing their skins over and over again so they suffer the most unbearable agony for all eternity.

I remember reading about a cruel Central Asian dictator who had Muslim rebels executed by boiling them alive in vats of scorching oil. I remember thinking what kind of insane monster would do that? Yet the Quran expects me to believe that God will not only do that – but will do it repeatedly. Preventing them from dying and replacing their skins so they endure this unimaginable agony forever. Not only did this contradict all reason, justice and mercy, it makes an utter mockery of the oft-repeated phrase: 'The Merciful the Compassionate'. In fact the Quran says God is not just merciful – he is 'The Most Merciful of those who show Mercy'. No amount of creative reasoning can ever square eternal torture with even an atom of mercy, let alone 'The Most Merciful of those who show Mercy'!

I usually responded to questions about Hell by saying: 'Oh it's just metaphorical', as do many Muslims. But now I had to admit that this didn't make sense either. Metaphor is a figure of speech in which a word or phrase is applied to an object or action to which it is not literally applicable. It doesn't change the meaning to something reasonable and acceptable. It means describing something using imagery that reflects that which is being described and aids our understanding of it. If I say: 'The room was a refrigerator', I mean it was abnormally cold. I don't mean it was a pleasant temperature. If one uses graphically grotesque endless torture as a metaphor, it means some sort of unimaginable suffering and agony. It cannot mean something benign. So whether unbelievers are to be literally burnt forever or it's a metaphor for some other inconceivable torment, the result it is exactly the same: A punishment that will cause unimaginable suffering and the most extreme pain possible, whether it be physical, mental or spiritual.

There now seemed no end of verses that I could no longer ignore. Verses that allowed slavery or cruel punishments such as flogging adulterers and amputating hands of thieves. I asked myself what was it about this book that made me believe it was the perfect word of God? The traditional claim is that the Quran is inimitable. However even if that were the case, the fact that something can't be imitated doesn't mean it's from God. However, now that I was reading it with a much more critical eye I could see flaws and weaknesses that were not apparent when I looked through the window of faith. The Quran is certainly excellent in parts but not so in others. It is also full of ambiguity and vagueness that the Quranic commentators have over the centuries struggled to explain.

A more modern defence of the Quran's supernatural nature is that it contains scientific miracles that were not known at the time. But again when I looked into each of these claims I found they were simply not true and are frankly just embarrassing. The more I read, the more I doubted.

The following verses addressed the pagans of Mecca who prayed to their idols for help. The Quran challenges them with a concrete test to prove their gods are false.

'Call on those whom you assert besides Him, they have neither the power to remove your troubles from you nor to change them.' (17:56)

'Who is more astray than he who calls on other than God, such as will not answer him?' (46:5)

'the things that you worship besides God have no power
to give you sustenance.' (29:17)

'Your Lord says: Call upon Me, I will answer you' (40:60)

'I answer the prayer of the supplicant when he calls on
Me' (2:186)

'(He it is) who answers the distressed one when he calls
upon Him and removes the evil.' (27:62)

But can't this test also be applied to God? Does God answer
prayers in any more direct way than the pagans believed their
gods did? I couldn't help thinking back to the nights I begged God
to save my baby daughter Huda and how I – like most Muslims
– made a thousand and one excuses for God for his apparent
lack of response. Don't the idols of the pagans also deserve a
thousand and one excuses for their apparent lack of response?

I had kept my doubts and views to myself apart from
some discussions with my two brothers. Then out of the blue
I received a text from my eldest sister. It read: *'How u doing?
I heard startlingly that u r becoming an apostate! Maybe u should
try 2 get hold of american writer – jeffry lang's "help i'm losing my
religion" love xx'*. Seeing the word apostate made my heart skip
a beat. I put the phone quickly back in my pocket. I told myself
that I shouldn't reply as sharing my thoughts would only upset
my sister. But the truth was I still couldn't admit to myself that I
no longer believed the Quran was the word of God. According
to traditional beliefs this made me an apostate. One can't reject
the divinity of the Quran and still be a Muslim. At least that
is what we are always taught. I felt I had no choice – I must
be an apostate. Although it was something I found difficult to
accept. Apostates are considered the lowest form of life by many
Muslims. They are seen as wilfully and sinfully turning away after
having being given the blessing of truth. They have arrogantly
rejected God and chosen disbelief over belief.

But one cannot simply *choose* to believe or disbelieve. I no longer believed the Quran was the word of God. I wasn't evil or bad or wilfully turning away. I had struggled with it long and hard. I had attempted over many years to make sense of problematic passages but I had to admit in all honesty the answers I found didn't satisfy me intellectually, spiritually nor morally. In fact, it was my belief that God would be better than this that gave me the courage to trust myself. I believed that if there is a God, the last thing he would want me to do was ignore the heart and mind he gave me – limited or not. He would want me to be honest and call it as I see it – even if I was wrong. He would surely appreciate honesty and sincerity as well as recognise our limitations – which after all he created us with.

It came as quite a relief when I finally went public with my views. In fact, I felt reinvigorated. I wanted to shout from the rooftops that the Quran is not God's perfect word. That religions were man-made. I felt like the child in *The Emperor's New Clothes* watching the naked procession, eager to tell everyone they've been duped. I accepted the label Ex-Muslim – albeit reluctantly as it didn't make sense identifying as an ex-something, rather like a person introducing himself as an ex-alcoholic. But I recognised that the label could be useful to others who were having doubts and like me felt alone and isolated. It would help break the taboo on leaving Islam and I had always believed that people should be free to be open about what they believe without fear of intimidation, abuse, or violence. I had never met anyone who had rejected Islam in real-life – at least not anyone who was open about it. But after searching on the internet I began to realise there were many others and I began to build some friendships – in particular with a Moroccan Ex-Muslim woman whose difficult and traumatic story moved me to tears. I felt I had to do something practical and I began making YouTube videos critiquing aspects of the Quran and Islam.

A few months later I saw Maryam Namazie, the Human Rights campaigner, announcing the formation of the Council of Ex-Muslims of Britain on the News. I immediately contacted her and told her I wanted to join to help and suggested an online forum could offer a safe place to support ex-Muslims who are unable to come out in public. Maryam agreed and with the help of my Moroccan friend we set up the Council of Ex-Muslims online forum for ex-Muslims and freethinkers to express themselves and find support.

I spent about four years with the Council of Ex-Muslims, attending debates, discussions, and campaigns with Maryam and others. Arguing for freedom of thought and conscience and an end to Shari'ah Law and Shari'ah councils. However, my own personal journey did not stop there – and although I still support Maryam's work and stand by the videos I made, I became increasingly uncomfortable with the label ex-Muslim and decided to drop it. I toyed with the label Agnostic Muslim, thinking that perhaps I could help bring about reform and do my bit to help Muslims. But I grew tired of this label too and eventually decided to dispense with labels entirely.

I'm just me. Hassan. A mixture or all the influences in my life. Islam being one of those influences – even though I no longer believed nor regarded it as divine. It was actually quite liberating to feel that I could freely pick and choose what wisdom I wish from Islam and discard that which I disagree with, openly and unashamedly without any of the ridiculously tenuous and disingenuous apologetics that progressive and liberal Muslims have been forced into because they refuse to let go of the idea of a perfect and divine Quran. There is wisdom in the words of the Quran. It is not divine wisdom. It is human wisdom. Like all thinkers of the past Muhammad felt inspired. Inspired in a very human and flawed sense. Humans are the active agents – not gods.

If there is a God, he is silent in all this. It is we humans who look up to the heavens and speak for God. We speak words limited by human nature and tied to our context. If religions are to survive beyond the twenty-first century they must evolve, just as humanity continues to evolve. If they cannot then they will die out. As the Quran itself says: 'As for the foam it passes away as a worthless thing but as for that which benefits mankind, it endures on the earth.' (13:17)

DOROTHY'S HIJAB

JIMMY BANGASH

The twenty-first century belongs to women of Muslim heritage.

This hundred years will see them claim their rightful place within the world. Fuelled with unrelenting strength and honed by unwavering resilience they shall destroy Islamic patriarchy.

Everywhere, men who were indoctrinated with the belief that women should be controlled will begin to reconnect with the injustice they felt as children, when they witnessed their sisters being caged.

The Gathering Waters

Two robed elderly men sit upon a high cliff looking out to sea, rainclouds dismissed, a rainbow heralds sunshine across the land beneath a bright blue sky. Grey beards fall over plain robes rippling gently in the wind.

'Is it so, Noah?' Abraham asks in an angry tone, legs crossed beneath him.

'See there,' Noah contemplatively points at the beach far below, perched on the edge, calves resting on the cliff face 'the waters are receding. For years now the tide does not come in.'

Abraham turns to face him sensing there is something more.

'But more than this, I hear her in the winds. The mother has awakened and her fury,' he shakes his head, 'it cannot be bound.'

'We *shall* bind her again!' Abraham gestures. Stretching the black niqab[1] taught between his hands.

'You have grown deaf, Abraham, and we have grown old', fatalism takes his voice. 'We did not stop her. She is gathering a tsunami and no ark I can build will save us. We thought her bound? She was merely watching. This time, she means to wash us away.'

He pauses, regret shapes his countenance, with quivering lips he whispers:

'We must submit.'

Pushing himself off the cliff he falls. Body plummeting with inevitable velocity, it crashes onto the rocks below, neck skewed at an unnatural angle.

Swiftly, eager waves crash upon the beach to claim him, pulling him into their watery depths.

Honour

'And tell the believing women to lower their gaze, and protect their private parts and not to show off their adornment except only that which is apparent, and to draw their veils all over and not to reveal their adornment except to their husbands ... And let them not stamp their feet so as to reveal what they hide of their adornment. And all of you beg Allaah to forgive you all, O believers, that you may be successful.' (Quran: *al-Noor 24:31*)

I am standing by the radiator in the hallway near the front door, waiting for my sister. My small 10-year-old hands feeling the raised floral print on the white wall paper, the pattern endlessly repeated from floor to ceiling, from front door to kitchen. White

---

[1] A veil worn by some Muslim women in public, usually black, covering all of the face apart from the eyes.

flowers on white paper, purity lost in meaningless repetition, relegated to banal existence by an absence of diversity.

Smiling, I note that I can now see down the back of the radiator. This is a recent occurrence. Only months ago my height precluded the discovery of the secrets that hid behind her. The radiator runs low to the floor, so attempts to place my head against the carpet and gaze up and under were thwarted. Undeterred by time, I knew this day would come.

On tip-toes, peering over the top of the white corrugated radiator; white like raised flowers on white walls, I am greeted by a richness of rustic brown. A welcome contrast. The radiator reveals to me that her back is not entirely painted. Silver mixed with brown and then a topping of white, the latter an attempt to keep the front and back consistent in appearance to the casual observer. I begin to pick away the white paint at the top of her back, allowing her more room to show herself and her majestic hues. Knowing that I am breaking some rule; I continue undeterred.

As flakes of paint fall to the ground I make a mental note that I must throw away the evidence so none of my family discovers this act of vandalism.

My sister is taking long. Only minutes ago she mentioned that she had spare travelcards and she asked if I wanted to go to London Bridge with her and look at the river. I eagerly accepted and she told me to wait downstairs while she gets ready.

I am excited. Though we live in London I have never been to London Bridge. Did I go once with school? More white flakes fall to the ground. Nonetheless I have never been invited to go out with my sister and I idolise her. She is the second oldest in our family and she teaches me and my siblings our maths homework. Her grasp of words in the English language encourages me to read more so that one day I can be as articulate as her and she says that she will study 'the law'. She is the most intelligent amongst us. I know she will be a judge because it is an important thing in 'the law'.

On occasion she will have a female friend come over from one of the neighbour's houses. Both my sisters share a room and their friend will join them. Sometimes, on very rare occasions, I am allowed to sit with them; if I am very quiet they let me stay, but mostly I am told to leave the room so they can speak with their friends in private. None of my older brothers are allowed to stay in my sister's room, nor do they seem to want to.

Footsteps on the stairs announce my sister's decent. I swiftly pivot and descend from my tip toes allowing my heels to cover the white flakes of paint on the floor. We smile at each other and I am assured my crimes have gone unnoticed.

She is wearing Hi-Tec trainers and black leggings with a jumper on top; the jumper is loose and hangs below her knees. Her hair is loose and falls across her back and shoulders. Lightened by streaks of 'Sun-In', which she tells me I am 'too young to use, but maybe one day'. My sisters are beautiful. I know they are. And somehow I know that they are popular too.

'Are you ready?' she asks

I nod in reply. I am in my shorts and t-shirt as the day is sunny and the breeze pleasant.

As she reaches for the latch on the front door the white living room door swings in and my brother steps into the hall-way. His rotund frame turning to face us, noting my sister, over my head he asks:

'Where are you going?'

There is something in his tone that indicates that our destination is not what he seeks to address. I shift my feet, pressing my heel in an attempt to crush white flakes of paint into small pieces so that they are invisible to the eye.

'We've got some travelcards for free so I'm gonna take Jimmy to London Bridge', my sister replies.

'You can't go out like that.'

'Like what?' she asks.

'Dressed like *that*. I can see your legs.'

The radiator and I take a moment to gaze at my sister. It is true, we confirm; my sister has legs, both of which can be seen. Such astute observations make me wonder whether I need bother crush the white paint any further. A part of my mind giggles at my sardonic wit. The rest is struggling to understand how things have become tense so swiftly. I am not entirely clear about the source of the tension.

'You can't see anything!' exclaims my sister.

'I can see your legs!' he says again, this time pointing.

His stumpy finger indicates that it is the appearance of ankle that is the issue. The gap between the trainer's collar and the end of the legging leaves approximately one inch of flesh exposed. Multiplied by two. Two inches. Calculations complete, I look up at my sister wondering if she will return upstairs to put on some socks in an effort to mitigate this travesty.

'Come on, Jimmy, let's go!' she states and moves to turn her back to my brother and open the front door.

My brother shouts, 'You can't go out like that! I'm gonna tell Dad and if you go out with her, Jimmy, I'm gonna tell Dad you went with her too!'

Time decides to linger.

White flecks of paint stir beside my feet, they melt into white fluid and gather together, slowly they coagulate and take form. Five liquid pillars of white rise from the floor, they form behind my brother as they morph into the shape of Islam's men. White turbans upon bearded faces, beards glistening with oil, their bodies covered in white robes. Behind them in the kitchen I see black, mournful shapes huddled together, rippling like the surface of an oil slick, impotent, lacking agency, tossed about by the sea.

The men gather behind my brother and begin reciting

incantations of Quranic script. It starts slowly in a single deep low Arabic voice and then the others join. Their pace and fever increase and the mournful mass in the kitchen begins to sway in time to the rhythm of their invocation.

'Bennnd ssssissster', the black mass whispers softly, words that slide beneath the dominating male hum. 'Lissssssssten', they hiss. 'Ssssuccumb.' Their serpentine sounds slither across the carpeted floor and reach my sisters feet coiling around her legs seeking to pull her to her knees and sap her resolve.

The presence of the men emboldens my brother's stance. As they lean closer to him the arm with which he points is strengthened, his back is straighter and shoulders squared. A translucent slab of force the size of my sister emits from him, pushing against her, more brazen and overt than the words that coil around her legs. It seeks to crush her will.

A third pitch raises from the hum, angelic, seeking to entice me with all the sweetness of a river full of honey; the men call to me as one of their own. They offer power and dominion over women. A lifetime where I am granted servitude. Sisters cleaning up after me, wives to fulfil my wishes and a paradise full of women whose numbers are so numerous men will die to reach them.

Such charms fail to lure me. I am inoculated from their spells by something more intrinsic.

I step backward between the barrier my brother has cast and reach for my sister's hand.

Time accelerates.

My sister grabs my hand and throws a look of disgust at my brother. She opens the door in no particular hurry and gently guides me in front of her. Looking back over her shoulder she says:

'Shut up you idiot. Tell Dad whatever you want!'

As she steps out of the door her back foot kicks up specks of white paint behind her.

The summer breeze greets us. Whilst we walk down the streets, hands held, I wonder if I will ever be as tall as her.

The Guardians

Abu Hurayrah (may Allah be pleased with him) reported that the Prophet Muhammad (blessings and peace of Allah be upon him) said: 'It is not permissible for a woman who believes in Allaah (God) and the Last Day to travel the distance of one day, except with a mahram (guardian).'

(Hadith Al Muslim – #1339)

Pretty soon my feet will reach the ground I think to myself looking down at the expanse between them and the foot mat. Reaching for the oppressive seat belt that allows me to be seated in the front by my father, I steady myself as he lowers his large stern frame into the seat. The beige Datsun Cherry shakes somewhat under his weight and lays closer to the ground. He is very tall and his feet reach the floor. Pedals bow low paying homage to his arrival.

It is sunny today and we are going on an outing. My father has said we are going to collect my eldest sister from college. I pump both arms to wind down the window as he turns the ignition. The car hums awake and as we reverse the descending slope of our sandstone drive way the fan belt beings to shriek. I am accustomed to this shrill noise and know that it will stop after a while.

'Sunrise radio, Fun-rise radio, Bilkul number One-rise Radio!' announce the car speakers in an Indian accent as my father switches on his favourite radio station. I squirm on the beaded seat covering, discomforted by the cacophony of noise. Much of my life is suffocated by languages I cannot understand. The joy in Indian music is less oppressive than the solemn Quranic recitations I am often exposed to so I am only momentarily disconcerted.

I have never been to a college and I wonder how big it will be and how many millions of people there will be there. Will there be books everywhere? Dusty tomes stacked upon each other in vast libraries where studious individuals sit on wooden benches peering over manuscripts, quietly learning all the knowledge of the world. Grey-robed librarians replacing returned books in alphabetical order, categorising, sombre and sagacious.

The tick-tock and green flashing light of the car's indicator on the dashboard penetrates my reverie and I vaguely hear my father say something about not getting out of the car.

How will they greet us when we arrive? Surely my intelligent sister will be well noted in this archaic institution. As we step up to knock the huge looming doors we will announce to the attendee that we are her kin and he will provide us with honorary treatment. The staff will coo over me as adults always do and they will note the intelligence in my eyes and comment that it will not be long before I too will be allowed to study there. I will hold a librarian's hand as she shows me around explaining how books are ordered. She will note my keen interest and ability to understand and my sister shall beam smiles of pride at my comprehension, advanced beyond its years.

We have been driving for days now, one hundred, maybe two hundred days. The alternating kicking of my feet is no longer amusing and the pressure of the seat belt against my chest an unwelcome trade for novel experiences. I sigh. The car slows down and my father takes on that focused look drivers wear when they are looking for parking. I sit up. Some way in the distance is a large building with steps leading up to it. Neither as grand nor antiquated as my musings, yet my enthusiasm returns. Some three million people are pouring out of its doors. People of all heights and colours who look remarkably ordinary. They are smiling and laughing and holding bags and rucksacks. Their energy is infectious and I embrace it.

My sister steps out of the door smiling and conversing and I immediately recognise her hair. In one dexterous move I unbuckle the seat belt, push open the parked car door and jump onto the pavement. My father says something but I spin and use my body's momentum to push the giant door closed on his words. My legs begin pumping and I sprint for miles and miles towards my sister. As I get to the foot of the stairs a sign declares 'Kilburn College'. Running up the gigantic stairs, needing both feet to ascend each step I shout my sister's name.

Her energy shifts immediately. The smile falls from her face and her lips stop moving.

As she kindly extends her hand out to take mine her eyes are peering over my head looking out in the direction I have come. Her eyes are strained. They are seeking, assessing, searching. Bemused by her greeting my energy subdues and wanes. There is cautiousness to my sister. She is wary, like something … hunted. Unable to identify the danger she senses I tug at her hand to gather her focus on me. She smiles down at me, eyes devoid of light and leads me down the steps.

'See you tomorrow, in the morning', one of the boys beside us on the steps says to her.

'Yeah, bye', like a ventriloquist she replies, without moving her mouth or turning her head. The boy is handsome so I turn to face him as my sister is walking down the steps and I wave boldly at him and say goodbye. He laughs.

A subtle increase in tension is displayed in my sister's eyes and in the almost imperceptible tightening of her grip on my hand. I do not understand. She walks faster now and keeps the veneer of a smile on her face. I realise that this is as good as her mood will get and begin my barrage of questions. How many people does she study with? How big is her college? What is a Kilburn? Are they extinct?

She begins to answer my questions on the swift walk back to the car but her presence is not within her voice, the jovialness in her laughter is feigned and she is walking too straight and too purposeful whilst attempting to look at ease. Her hand is warmer. This would be unnoticeable to most but I myself have become habituated to monitoring and managing my own body, voice and gaze. This façade is one I am accustomed to donning and I recognise it immediately.

Beige Datsun Cherry door before me, she tells me to get into the front seat. As she is older I naturally defer the seat to her, but she declines. Some rule I do not understand regulates that I will always sit in front of her. I clamber in and beam a smile at my father. The smile is not returned, his reconnaissance plan sabotaged by an excitable child. He is stern and sombre. My sister lowers herself into the seat behind me whilst offering her Salaams, placing her bag beside her. I have more questions but there is a combustible oppression within the car which stifles conversation. As though at any moment the air might ignite.

We begin to drive in silence. My father's eyes look into the rear-view mirror and meet my sister's gaze. Loaded with gravitas he asks:

'Who was that boy?'

Muslim women are cloth.

Dupatta[2] layered over kameez[3] which hangs low over loose fitting salwar[4].

Mothers frayed and worn by time, colours faded by

---

[2] A length of material worn arranged in two folds over the chest and thrown back around the shoulders, or worn draped over the head to cover hair.

[3] A long tunic by worn many women in South Asia.

[4] A pair of light, loose, pleated trousers, usually tapering to a tight fit around the ankles, usually covered in front and back by a kameez.

selflessness and adversity. Threadbare fingers spinning Singer sewing machines in East London flats. Working, working, working. Needles stitching dignity and pride into generations of family tapestry, suppressed by toxic masculinity.

Grannies cast in worn white cotton, sitting cross-legged folding clothing. Ironing creases out of garments transferred by rising stream onto their faces. Deep crevices. Tan like leather armour cured in the sun, nicked and marked by patriarchal blows to which they have long since surrendered any dreams or desires of their own.

Young girls are silks and satins, hymens tightly wrapped and coiled around fabric bolts, stacked on high shelves, out of reach. Bold colours alluring and enticing, glistening and smooth to the touch. Fathers and brothers police their sheen, seeking to extinguish the flame of sexuality that burns within them. Guarded by men for men they are brought down to be fawned over when aunties are seeking brides for precious sons. Silently they yearn to be unfurled, cut and set free.

Ofttimes they *are* cut. Virginity commoditised and exchanged for matrimony.

Unwaveringly, seemingly nonchalant, in Pashto she replies, 'Just some boy who is in my class.'

She searches in her bag for nothing.

Obedience

'Men are the maintainers of women because Allah has made some of them to excel others and because they spend out of their property; the good women are therefore obedient, guarding the unseen as Allah has guarded; and (as to) those on whose part you fear desertion, admonish them, and leave them alone in the sleeping-places and beat them; then if they obey you, do not seek a way against them; surely Allah is High, Great.' (Quran: *An-Nisa 4:34*)

Within her eyes all sound and sight ceases. Viscous oils welcome me with their aroma. They flow and engulf me in peace, silence, serenity. Darkness and the welcome succour of sleep lull me into – I am jolted back to light. My face wet?

Sound and sight come flooding back. An unwelcome assault on my mind.

In front of me mum screams loudly as my father twists her arm behind her back pressing the axe against her neck yelling he will kill her.

I am paralysed with fear. Against the wall of the house in our back garden; terror holding me in place even as I want to run to help her. Tears stream down my face.

Somewhere to my right, (beside the butterfly tree?) siblings cry, screaming in Pashto[5]:

'NO! STOP!'

They daren't move.

The wind howls 'Sacrilege!' The garden is *her* space.

Her free arm flails to protect her and push away the blade but he yanks and twists her arm forcefully. She screams for the neighbours but her cries are absorbed by the long silence of community.

He tries to press the axe to her throat again and her long black hair is tossed about by the wind as they struggle.

I wail loudly and my body begins to shudder. Legs shaking, arms trembling. Please, Allah, no.

He is choking her now. Large Pashtun hands gripping her throat. As she is gasping her head turns frantically seeking me out, our eyes lock …

… Desperate twin hazel olive pools pull me to their depths, charming and enveloping, I drown within their waters. Sight and sound fall away as she casts her spell of slumber. I smell saffron

[5] An Iranian language spoken in Afghanistan and Pakistan; the official language of Afghanistan.

and turmeric, both greet me with their warmth. Stirring me in circular motions with a worn, wooden spoon. Falling now, falling deep past hob and stove I land cushioned on white beds of flour, my impact sending up above me clouds of flour dust. Smiling as my legs give out beneath me, back sliding down against the wall, from somewhere the sweet scent of kheer.

Far, far away; at the edges of my consciousness howling winds bear aloft the prayers of Muslim children, wishing death upon their father.

The people of Lot

And (remember) Loot (Lot), when he said to his people: 'Do you commit the worst sin such as none preceding you has committed in the 'Aalameen (mankind and jinn)?' (al-A'raaf 7:80)

I hate myself. Each day I loathe myself. I wish that I were dead.

I am in a mosque outside London and I have come away for a weekend retreat. None of my family have come with me but as I am a teenager now and some elders from my local mosque have come, my father gave consent. Subscription to these retreats has become a more frequent occurrence now that I have come to accept that I am gay. The irony of being segregated with the gender you are attracted to but forbidden from loving is not lost on me.

Barefoot, I step into the ablution area to perform my Wudu.[6] Small green, blue and turquoise tiles form mosaic patterns across the walls. Circles, triangles, pentagons interlace weaving into collective shapes that dwarf their individualism. Each tile

---

[6] The Islamic ritual washing to be performed in preparation for prayer and worship.

insignificant within the collective it has been called to serve, stationary and dutiful they contribute to the whole in rich conformity. Six taps protrude from the walls with corresponding granite cuboid stools. Each an identical copy of the other. As I lower myself to the seat I take a breath to centre myself and turn on the tap. Water flows before me and I cup it in my left hand and use it to wash my right. 'Bismillah'[7] I recite each time. Three times right hand then three times left. 'Bismillah, Bismillah'.

For years now I have prayed that these waters would wash away my homosexuality. Calling on the divine to purge me of this malady. At first when I became aware that I was attracted to other guys at school in the same way that they were attracted to the girls, I rejected the reality. I would tell myself that I wasn't attracted to them and that it was just that I wanted to be like them or wanted to be friends with them. That ruse could only be maintained for so long. Intelligence provides little compatibility with denial. An absence of interest in women, even when I forced myself to date them, corroborated the lust I felt for men.

I rinse my mouth three times and then proceed to rinse my nose. Allah does not favour the prayers of those who rush and pray by rote. He commands attentiveness to devotion. The empty washroom means I do not need to accelerate my pace and there is plenty of time before prayer.

'Bismillah.' Hands cupped together I catch water from the tap and proceed to wash my face.

Fire. Burning fire greets my face and body. Searing the flesh and melting it so that it falls to the molten earth beneath my feet. I am forced to eat vegetation that catches in my throat choking me, thorns twisting and piercing and all the while I scream. The liquid blood and pus that falls from my immolated flesh is fed to me, eagerly I drink desperate for respite but pain, colossal,

---

[7] Arabic. Translation: 'In the name of God'.

unspeakable pain racks my body whilst my throat and innards burn from searing liquids. Falling on my front somehow I wail; 'Mercy!' Giant guardian angels strike my head pounding my body into burning earth, crushing bone and brain and skull. The solace of death and oblivion eschewed as I am wrenched back to my feet, my body renewed to be eternally tortured and cast in flames again.

'Bismillah.' Deftly with practiced skill I cup water in my right hand and elevate my arm so that the water runs down my forearm. The dexterity involved in this manoeuvre has made it my favourite part of ablution. Three times right and three times left. 'Bismillah.'

Shame. Deep, deep, shame. And sadness. I have learned to hide my malady. Cautious in every waking moment of my life, assessing how it manifests and then altering my behaviour to negate it. Sitting with friends sometimes I wish to cross my legs and must remember to place the outside of my heel on my knee rather than crossing one thigh over the other. When meeting or speaking to men, or even observing them I am conscious of how long I may have looked at them and ensure that it does not convey any semblance of the attraction that I may feel. I am uncomfortable in the company of men now; their presence is a constant reminder of this test or punishment I have been given and I find myself far more able to be myself amongst women. Fortunately, I am in a mixed gendered college and this allows me to make female friends. Bizarrely this increased time around women facilitates a stigma of homosexuality.

I monitor myself this way because I am present to the impact the discovery of this truth will have upon my family. The punishment for homosexuality is death, and whilst I have not partaken in the act I know I cannot maintain this abstinence forever. Islamic homosexuality is intrinsically linked with fear, death and violence and I worry for my safety. I am certain I will be disowned.

'Bismillah.' Head, ears, feet all washed I proceed past empty shoe racks to the mosque hall. The carpet is covered in maroon and cream geometric shapes that form identical alcoves; space for ten men to stand side by side and space for at least as many rows. A Muslim brother once told me the geometric points represent the Mihrab[8] in a mosque pointing towards Mecca.

Lowering myself to sit upon the carpet my mind races back to a recent memory in my mother's bedroom. I am sat upon the carpet reading a novel and in the background the television talk show host introduces the first guest. He is gay and intends to tell his mother and brother about his sexuality on the show. My body stiffens and immediately I scan to check and release any tension in my face and shoulders whilst ensuring nothing visibly moves. I want to put down my book but my own brother and mother are in the room and I do not wish to arouse suspicion with my attentiveness.

'Jimmy look at this!' an incredulous cry from my brother whilst pointing at the screen. I put down my book. My mother's limited grasp of English does not allow her to understand the show so she asks for a translation.

We have no word for gay. Filth, scum, sodomite, fag, pervert and asshole all congregate in the Pashto swear word 'Kuni'.[9] I am mindful that if I ever want to explain to my mother that I am gay I will have to swear at myself to do so. It is a word I've grown to loathe.

My brother explains the scenario and collectively from different angles and perspectives we watch the television. The family members are brought onto the set and the guest reveals his sexuality to them. His mother cries and his brother seethes in anger. Both try to

---

[8] A niche in the wall of a mosque, at the point nearest to Mecca, towards which the congregation faces to pray.

[9] Pashto swear word. Translation: Homosexual/Gay.

convince him that he isn't who he is. All the while, their English is being translated into Pashto by my brother to facilitate my mother's understanding, whilst I feign only mild interest.

I wonder at the cruelty of Allah's test and whether some sin I have committed has led him to punish me with this disease. This disease of the heart.

'He's disgusting!' my brother says. I reach to pick up my book. 'Don't you think?' my brother asks.

In this moment, my dignity resides as a sphere upon a fulcrum, precariously balanced and facing an inevitable plunge, prodded by this question. One answer plummets into familial safety and acceptance, birthdays, Ramadan and Eid. Security and financial stability steeped in a disingenuous existence. The other answer leads to a world of uncertainty, homelessness, isolation and abandonment beneath a sky of authenticity. As I look at the man upon the screen I realise *he* is my kin.

'I think he's brave,' I reply, 'incredibly brave.'

My brother sputters and the ensuing conversation which I refuse to engage in is an attempt to highlight the endless faults of gays linking them to bestiality, the cessation of the human species, Allah's condemnation of Lot's people, paedophilia, incest, and the signs of the end of the world:

Kuni are the dog faeces to be scraped off your shoe on the raised edge of the pavement.

Interestingly, despite several attempts by my brother to engage her, my mother resists being drawn into the conversation. Therefore, it does not last. I take my book and leave the room. Closing a door behind me.

The entrance of men into the mosque hall brings me back to this space but something within me has shifted. As I watch them line up side by side in solidarity, neatly in little spaces allocated to them, much like individual tiles in mosaic patterns, I am present to my difference.

Sliding up the wall I decide to leave and sit outside the mosque. Cars drive past and then stop at the red traffic light. Leaning on the wall, I listen to the music pouring from their speakers. Haram and so enticing.

Guitar chords strum whilst a woman voice sings, wrapping round my consciousness, she tugs. I resist and attempt to stay grounded in this place but her voice, it bequeaths trust. I surrender as she wraps me in melody, carrying me safely on her notes, gently she drops me into a future far away.

The night club is unfamiliar. Men are everywhere, clad in denim jeans with stylish belts that feature buckles. Few, very few wear tops, most are shirtless with muscular physiques moving and shaking to house music while consuming drinks. A tall man walks past me and our eyes meet, on his shoulder a superman tattoo. I smile as he turns towards me. He introduces himself and points to his hearing aid.

There are *deaf gays*!? I wonder to myself.

He is able to lip read and we spend some time talking. Somehow, he recognises a song and enticed by its lyrics he grabs my hand and pulls me onto the dance floor. His momentum draws me through the crowd and we reach a group of friends he introduces me to. Together, we all dance, swinging arms and hips and legs and singing to the tune.

'What's this club called?' I mouth the words to him.

'Heaven,' he replies.

Traffic lights turn green and cars begin to move, driving visions away.

'Jimmy, you wasn't in prayer, is everything okay?' one of the brothers asks.

'No, no I wasn't, and yes. Everything is going to be okay.'

Shadows

*It was narrated from Ibn`Abbas that the Messenger of Allah said:
'Whoever you find doing the action of the people of Lut, kill the
one who does it, and the one to whom it is done.'*

(Sunan Ibn Majah 3:20:2561)

The bright white page on the screen of the monitor fills with
black Times New Roman letters. Writing about Shakespeare's
plays for university enraptures me so that I forget the discomfort
of the keyboard being too high. My desk was once a dining table
for 4 and the chair I sit in is secondhand and made for comfort,
not desk work. The combination of the two is akin to eating at a
dinner table from your settee.

There is a knock at my closed bedroom door. It is always
closed. I push back the chair and move to open the door. Standing
slightly to the right of it is my oldest brother. I nod at him while
my mind is racing over how to construct the next paragraph in
my assignment.

'Can I come in and talk for a minute?' he asks reasonably. I
nod turning my back to him so he can follow me into the room
and I scratch a note on my pad. Concern about my assignment
alleviated, I turn the chair 180 degrees so its back is against the
table-desk; I seat myself and look up to see how I can help.

Tension.

Like a fool, captivated by my studies, I did not realise that two
more of my brothers had stepped into the room. They position
themselves, one in front and one on each side of me. These
are violent men. Their veins are full of misogyny and Islamic
supremacy, and I am afraid.

I do not know how – or if – I will escape this encounter. A
part of me chastises myself for taking a seat. I have now given
them the advantage of looming over me. From this position it

will be near impossible to defend myself. I should know better than to have dropped my guard in this house.

For at least a decade now I have known this moment would come. Living day by day towards an inevitable cataclysm that I am fated to experience. I have used the years to prepare.

I have never been this afraid, my mouth is dry and I do not know if they will try to kill me or merely assault me. If it is the later I wish to protect my face.

Forcing a friendly smile onto my face whilst shifting my position on the chair, I nonchalantly bring my knees in front of me whilst leaning to the side. The door is to the left and if I leap in that direction there is only one man to overcome. My older brothers are large and though I am in my early twenties I do not have their size. I shift my head to the right slightly, ensuring less light is caught in my eyes. Constricted pupils could be interpreted as fear and the scent of fear leads beasts to attack. Simultaneously I use my left hand to scratch the right side of my face allowing my forearm to cover my throat, while I swallow and reset my voice without them seeing. Gathering my breath, I ask, 'Is everything okay?'

Success. The pitch and tone of my voice belies no fear and carries genuine enquiry. I turn my head from right to left while asking, my face shifting to an inquisitive visage which seeks to include them all whilst I scan the room for weapons. Scissors, knife, anything.

'Who is Gavin?' the eldest asks.

Ice, so cold, like endless arctic tundra courses through my body. My heart beats faster and my body wants to quiver. I struggle to control panic, but I do not move.

Choosing a lower octave I reply, 'He is my friend.'

'Friend or boyfriend? We know you are gay!' He shouts whilst gesturing aggressively with his arm.

Too often have I seen these hands around my sister's throat

for besmirching honour or some Islamic ideal of modesty.

I resolve that at least one of them must die with me:

Muslim gays are Hashashin.[10]

Dark robed garments wrap around their bodies. Faces hidden behind cowls, cloaked in shadow and darkness as they meet in the night. Alley, park, sauna and car are the landscape upon which these ethereal figures entwine. Identities hidden even from each other, longstanding unspoken codes dictate anonymity and concealment. Deftly they meld into secrecy and silence; nameless, faceless apparitions.

In this darkness, amidst mounds of cloth, beneath nature's night, rain or winds, clandestine carnal encounters unfold. Huddled together, uncomfortably groping and thrusting, hands clumsily fumbling with buckles whilst lips yearn to kiss but resist. For kissing is blasphemy, an unbroken threshold, a segue to intimacy and reality. Lips must eschew and instead bite on necks or collar or jacket or shoulder where darkness reigns and shadows reside.

And then a grasp becomes firmer, uncomfortably real. One shadow elevates itself in the meld. Breath becomes quicker as it moves with more vigour bereft of concern for all others. A groan and swift climax. And then, slowly it comes … the pouring of deep deep shame into the void. Pushing away all contact, the shadow unfurls from the meld vowing (again) never to return. Thin frame scuttling from door frame to lamppost to car.

Hashashin dance in courts of intrigue, skilled in the web of subterfuge and deceit that they weave. Keys jingle in doors as they slide back into homes where children run to greet them. Lifting them high into the air they whirl them in circles. Lies upon lies upon wives that step out from kitchens, hands coated in flour as they smile and exchange kisses.

[10] Persian Assassins.

Hidden daggers sit at their waist. Ready to spill the blood of those that seek to spill their secrets.

'... disgusted that I have shared the same cutlery as you and drank from the same glass! It makes me sick!'

'Get out of this house!' my brother yells with an air of finality.

Five words that set me free.

Rebirth

'So you never ate the apple?' asks the little girl.

'No, child, I did not', replies Eve.

'But you told everyone you did?' asks another, a little older, confusion cast upon her youthful face.

'He wasn't able to confess, child. He took what was not his. Then, driven by shame and a fear of condemnation he came begging for aid at my door. I knew the others would not hurt me for I am The First.

'I decided to lie for him. I was young then and my compassion led me to such foolishness. I sought to provide him a second chance. Instead, for a hundred thousand years women were held responsible for every failing man ever had. Time passed and he convinced himself that I was to blame. Repeat a lie for long enough child and it will feel like the truth.

'I returned to Eden not long after and confessed. Here I have remained watching the world of men as they cut our womanhood from between our legs, sought to cover us in darkest fabric and held public stonings, slaying us for their inability to control their lust.

'It took time to gather the waters to my will but now I have washed them all away.'

'But there are still men? Some were admitted before The Great Wave?' queries the youngest.

'Indeed there are. The hue of their souls is more akin to our own than those that we submerged.

'No more questions for today, run along and find your mother, I saw her last with the Men of the Purple Hand.'

The children run off racing each other, luscious glistening hair trailing behind.

Eve walks towards a large, tall apple tree. Thick trunk worn with time, aged with sorrow and wariness. Branches shift slightly as she approaches, layering leaves over each other, providing a canopy that offers shade from the morning sun. Despite the sadness of this place she has grown to love it.

The melancholy of the apple tree provides a contrast that heightens the sounds of joy and laughter from the children that once again inhabit Eden. For too long were they gone, banished from her world.

Sitting cross legged, back against the trunk she focuses on her breath. Deep slow breaths that tie her to the land, connecting her with tree and grass and root. The power of this world is tied into The First and her exhalation is a calling to the wind. The breeze rustles leaves and grass blades bend low.

Summoning cosmic energies whist raising her right arm she traces a translucent pink triangle in the air in front of her, point facing to the ground. It hovers, pulsing with her breath, a conduit to siphon Eden's energy. Wrapping herself in eternal sustenance and power she begins to fortify her body.

For tomorrow she must lose another rib.

PURITY

MARWA SHAMI

I am not sure when I completely stopped believing in Islam. I started to struggle with believing in God, especially Islam's version of an omniscient, omnipotent, and omnibenevolent God, during my early teens. Endlessly I prayed, despite my doubts, and years went by while I begged for my life to get better. At some point I gave up on him, but I don't know exactly when the flame that I held for him dimmed away. His love is said to be seventy times more powerful than a mother's, but I couldn't believe that he loved me more than mine. She would never burn me repeatedly in the pits of hell no matter what I did. She would hardly be comfortable sitting in paradise with her loved ones burning repeatedly in hell. My kind mum would get nervous for me if I were caught out in the rain.

I think it is unbelievable the way confirmation bias is used whenever you try to ask a question that others find difficult to answer. I started to see Allah as an absent God who sent a flawed final message to humans to guide them through situations that are sometimes so unbearable. Islam was my life and it consumed me, so I became crippled with anxiety that there was something wrong with me for having these thoughts. In the Quran, those who do not believe are described as 'dumb deaf and blind' with darkness in their hearts. This made me see disbelief as some kind of disease, a virus which spreads through the body every time that you sin as you edge closer to the fires that will use human bodies writhing in pain as fuel. Every time I did something sinful, I felt like this virus was spreading all over my body and soul.

The severe warnings about transgressing sexual boundaries I heard from the Quran, Ahadeeth and Sunnah led me to have a fragile mind, riddled with self-persecution, where I felt isolated and not prepared for the doubts that I was to have. The things I was taught about Islamic concepts regarding gender, sex, love, and marriage during my early formative years still affect me, even though I stopped believing in Islam a long time ago. Shifting my views on ideological questions about whether Islam is true or not, was the easy part. Unlearning the toxic sexist narrative that I was taught and recovering from the impact that it has had on my sense of autonomy and self-esteem will be much harder.

As a child, I attended an ordinary state primary school in a middle-class suburb in London. I didn't care about the difference between girls and boys at that age; I wanted to play with everyone. In Year I, my best friend wore a headscarf and I wanted to be just like her, so I asked my parents if I could also wear it. My mother was delighted, and she found me a lovely blue one to match my uniform at school. Little did I know, that the hijab would end up representing the discrimination and prejudice that I would encounter for the rest of my life just because I am a woman. I couldn't know this apparent 'choice' that I made at the tender age of five to wear a hijab would be the first brick of the wall I that I had to put up to become a Muslim woman who had to accept that gender segregation was good for the fabric of society. I can't say that I was forced to wear the headscarf because in some ways it was my choice. I do however use the term 'choice' – loosely because I was only five years old and I had no concept of what it meant. My family were becoming increasingly religious at the time and they thought it was adorable. I was a child who wanted to earn my parents' approval in a hostile home. The positive reinforcement that I received from teachers, family members and anyone in my small close-knit community was enough to dislodge how uncomfortable the piece of cloth truly was. I had no real attachment to it. I find it hard to explain the extent to which covering my body impacted me; it made me realise that I was different because I was a woman and therefore an object of lust.

Gender segregation was of the utmost importance. Islam forbids the free mixing of men and women because it can lead to fitnah (meaning unrest and chaos) and ultimately illicit relationships. I felt a perverse amount of sexual attention while I went through puberty. I hardly dealt with the growth of my breasts, the deep curve of my waist, and the width of my hips before I was told to keep them covered under loose clothing. Why? Because it might attract attention and if 'something' happened, this would ruin my purity. So much blame was placed on me even when walking with a headscarf, and loose or long fitted clothing if there was a chance that a man could stare at the outline of my breasts. I was told off repeatedly for the actions of men who stared and made offensive sexual remarks. I was made aware that I was an object of desire before I had the opportunity to create my own sense of self and femininity. I was treated like a temptress who had to be hidden away. I could not confide in my family if men sexually harassed me. I felt shame for being a woman who must have brought it on herself.

As a teenager, I was kept away from men most of the time. For my high school education, I was sent to a small Islamic high school for girls. I was constantly reminded in school and at home that hijab was essential and that it was much more attractive for a woman to leave things to the imagination of men. I felt like a freak for receiving attention even while wearing a headscarf and loose dress. I was taught that women should wear hijab to help men to control their urges. It was not only a requirement for women but also a kindness towards men to protect them from the burning fires of hell. It unnerved me that men would stare at me especially as I was taught you could commit fornication with your eyes which is why unrelated men and women are told to keep their eyes on the floor when they see each other. I felt practically invisible as my school uniform at the time was a large plain black headscarf with the school's logo with a long loose black dress to my feet. There was nothing to look at, except my face and hands. I just blended into a shade of black. No colour, no joy, no individuality, just uniformity. I was plagued by a constant fear of being noticed by the other sex, to the point I would look down on the floor while walking, praying that my eyes did not catch another's, as this seemed to be enough consent for strange men to catcall or follow me. My thought patterns ran rancid with the belief that I should be punished if I ever felt a man gaze at me with what I understood to be lustful eyes, because I must have warranted it, and thus be blamed for it.

I had myself second-guessing every word, every movement, and every action around the other gender, even if they were male members of my extended family. I had had no issue interacting and having normal friendly conversations with males as a child; however, as I matured, constant warning from my mother about men drove me to panic about whether I was behaving in a morally loose way. I felt penalised for how my body had developed. I felt like I was an inconvenience for my family members because I grew to have a curvy hourglass figure. Hiding my shape under loose clothing did little to reassure me that there was nothing wrong with my body. I looked bigger than most of my peers as early as Year 8 because of how voluptuous I grew to be, which was obvious even in all the Islamic clothing. I became fixated on this, and with how it looked, which consequently led to an eating disorder.

I remember once losing more than a stone in less than two weeks because I spent all my time avoiding food, throwing up what I did eat and exercising for hours after school. But nothing I did made my breasts any smaller and I felt any sign of their true size would cause offense.

Although I was an active child who loved sports, I could not do the things that I wanted to do because I would have had to play with boys. I sometimes wonder how much it stunted my personal growth as someone who enjoyed football, running, swimming. I was prevented from taking gymnastic lessons because my parents forbade me from wearing a leotard, though I was only in primary school. I felt humiliated during my primary school swimming classes because I was made to wear leggings and a t-shirt because there were boys in my class. I loved the feeling of the water on my skin, but I could not enjoy my classes as I felt like an outsider. I couldn't explain to my non-Muslim teachers the turmoil it would cause at home if I tried to push back against my parents' choice of clothing for me. I did not want to cover my legs, my arms, or my shoulders, and the headscarf prevented me from taking part in the activities I wanted to do. It is no wonder that an eating disorder obsessed with control manifested. I wanted to slow down the process that was taking me into womanhood. My training to become a modest Muslim woman began so early. For me, the hijab took away my childhood and it will always be synonymous with lost opportunities.

The Islamic School that I attended for my high school education taught an orthodox Sunni interpretation of Islam. We were being prepared and taught how to fulfil our purpose by becoming good wives, child bearers and God-fearing women. We were taught in detail about the prophet Muhammad and his wives. Some of the things that we were taught were not appropriate for school-age children in my view. We were taught that these were stories with clear instructions on how we should live.

My Islamic studies teacher was a shrewd and pretty woman who used to tell us how much she would love to have a husband like Muhammad. She said he was a beautiful warrior who served in the way of God. It did not sit right with me to want to be with a man who engaged in that level of violence, who did not end slavery and had more than one wife, though four is the limit proscribed for Muslim men. I was taught very distinctively that men were allowed more than one wife, that this was indisputable and not sufficient grounds to ask for a divorce. A woman's consent for her husband to marry another woman is not a prerequisite for a man to take another wife in Islam. We were taught that we were not allowed to question stories that led to the creation of laws that discriminate against millions of women across the world. In fact, we were taught that it was not misogynistic for a man to be able to take multiple wives where women were not extended the same rights, because Islamic law comes from God and therefore must be good for the social order.

One story that I was taught made me feel confused and uncomfortable was about Aisha. We were taught that the prophet's youngest wife was six years old at the age of marriage and nine years old when he had sexual relations with her. This did not strike me as strange during those years because we were also taught that girls matured faster 1400 years ago, particularly in hot climates, so a nine-year-old child was more like an eighteen-year-old woman now – even though there is no science which backs this. We were taught that their story was another example of how married couples should behave. Aisha was once accidentally separated from Muhammad and his companions when they travelled away from home. She was found by one his followers, Safwan bin Muattal, and he took her safely home. During the time that she was away, a rumour that she had slept with Safwan began to circulate. No one told her that this rumour was spreading, however it is said that she noticed that her husband, the supposed prophet, was acting strangely towards her. Very soon after she learnt about the rumours from her parents, verses of the Quran were revealed to Muhammad that absolved her of the crime of adultery.

What strikes me about this story is that Muhammad is supposed to be an example for all men on how to be good husbands, yet he did not even approach her to ask her what had happened while she was lost in the desert and assumed that she might have had an affair. This story highlighted to me that even the wife of the prophet wasn't safe from the constant surveillance and suspicion that follows women around in case they do something that would threaten their purity. I find it upsetting to think that if the story were true, she would have only been fourteen years old at the time. It was hardly appropriate for a class of twelve-year-olds to discuss the possible infidelity of a child bride. However, this is what we considered to be normal.

I was taught that as women we needed to be patient and place our trust in our Lord. If we questioned or doubted, these thoughts were coming from a place of evil and were the whisperings of the devil in our ears. It was not just about the example of prominent women during the prophet's life that we were taught to follow. The male companions of Muhammad during his life were also held up as people that we should aspire to be like. One of his followers frightened me. His name was Umar bin Al-Khataab and he was the father of Hafsa, one of Muhammad's wives. He was a harsh man who was once reported to have slapped his daughter because she and the other wives complained about the poverty that came with being a wife of the prophet. During one of our classes, we learned about a story where a man was unhappy with one of Muhammad's rulings and that he challenged it first by going to Muhammad's right-hand man Abu Bakr, who also happened to be a brother-in-law and the father of the youngest wife, Aisha. Abu Bakr told that man that he accepted the prophet's decision and so the man went to Umar bin Al-Khataab next. It was narrated that Umar emerged with the man's head after killing him for his disobedience and unwillingness to accept Muhammad's ruling. Although some argue that this narration is not 'authentic', it was taught to me when I was a teenager as though it were historical fact. The violence of this story gave me chills; to think that a man would be beheaded for asking for a second opinion.

Even though it made me uncomfortable, I was taught that I should not question or doubt this, and accept that he deserved it for challenging the prophet's decision. My feelings and opinions were dismissed and pushed aside. I was not to question things because, as a young person, I was unable to understand the truth of these stories or how these righteous people acted. This was how I reassured myself when I was taught about the battles that took place and the nameless slave women who were captured on the mission to spread the word of God. It wasn't that this was wrong; I simply did not have the capacity to understand. There are verses in the Quran that instruct Muslim men about their slave women captured after war, and none say to end the oppression and suffering of women completely. We were not supposed to feel sorry for Saffiyah, the Jewish wife of Muhammad who was captured after members of her family and tribe were killed during the Battle of Khaybar. We are told that she was taken from her home after this bloody event, with a veil over her to signify that she was not a captured slave and that she became one of the wives of Muhammad. I am not sure which woman would willingly consent to marry the man who led the army that killed her father, especially so soon after the event.

My teachers revered Muhammad and to question his morals was too much of a taboo. The stories of Muhammad and his wives were presented to me as great, ideal romantic stories, and yet why did it feel so wrong? I kept my concerns and sympathy for his wives to myself, because the horror that I felt did not seem to be shared by my teachers or classmates. I spent some time trying to look for an alternative understanding of Islam because I could not suppress my distaste for what I was being taught at school. I used a popular forum on the Internet that had many members who were young Muslims like me seeking answers. These users were from all over the world. Suddenly I became uninterested in the Islam being taught at school when I realised that there could be another way to understand my religion. I sought answers online because I felt too afraid to speak to anyone at school or at home. It didn't matter how many questions I asked, or how many adult Muslim men I spoke to online from the age of twelve, I had critical issues with Islam, which could not be answered in a way that could convince me that my religion wasn't full of huge, gaping holes. This was the beginning of a pattern that would emerge in my romantic life later, where I would turn to my Muslim lovers to answer my questions. I believed that men held a certain authority and if anyone was going to be able to deal with my doubts, it would be a man.

As I reached maturity, I did the one thing that I was trained not to do, as I fell into the temptation of men. I was taken out of the Islamic school that I was attending in the last year of high school for various reasons, including the fact that it became obvious to my family that my mental health was suffering there. After years of segregation, I was at an ordinary high school where I was petrified of the other sex. I was not prepared to speak to them and every small interaction left me feeling nervous. I thought that they only saw me as a sexual object and I found it hard to form any kind of relationship with them. At this point in my life, I did remove my headscarf. It was accepted without any real opposition from my parents because I was obviously very unhappy and I had the support of my older siblings. Readjusting in a new and normal environment with my peers being from a slightly more diverse background, I was anxious and the segregation I was used to did little to teach me how to have normal conversations with men. I always felt like they had an ulterior motive, something sexually perverse. I was so unsure of myself, and spent a lot of time avoiding male attention wherever possible.

As the months passed, I found a way to try to fit in and some of my anxiety passed. At the age of seventeen I met my first boyfriend. He was handsome, with lovely brown skin and he was from a respectable Muslim family. He ticked my boxes … which I later came to realise were not actually my boxes, but rather my family's. As we started to date we both made it clear that we couldn't have sex until we were married. It became an important part of our relationship to discuss marriage, even though we weren't a good match and were so young. Although I had become agnostic about religion, I was obsessed with the notion of marriage seeing it as the only way that I could have romantic relationships or explore my sexuality.

Every kiss and touch, made me feel less of a woman, less pure because it happened outside marriage, and I could not even bring myself to repent. Eventually I started to self-harm due to a range of factors, including guilt about having a boyfriend. One of the ways that I used to hurt myself was by burning my skin. I believe that the constant reminder that even if you die a Muslim, you would be sent to Hell first to be cleansed of your sins, fuelled this type of self-harm. I was one of those young Muslims who felt tormented by the horrors of the hereafter. Still, I couldn't help myself from falling in love. I was so sheltered that I believed that the first man I slept with had to be my husband and the way that I justified the illicit relationship to myself was that we had promised each other that we would get married one day. I think that he meant it at the time but we were innocent and naive. He knew about my doubts and we would spend hours arguing about Islamic theology. He was to become the first of a string of Muslim boyfriends who would feel excited by the prospect of bringing me back to Islam.

Eventually we both gave in and committed the natural act of sex. Even though I felt like the same person, losing my virginity and what happened afterwards, cast a shadow over my life for some time. He broke up with me a few weeks later saying that I wasn't Muslim enough for his family and that we couldn't get married. What hurt more than anything else was that he spent a large amount of time crying about how guilty he felt for 'ruining' my purity. As far as he was concerned, he saw me as damaged goods and he wanted to apologise for being the one to do this to me. It became apparent to me that I was stuck in a Catch-22 situation when it came to relationships. I couldn't be with a non-Muslim like myself and yet I was not good enough for Muslim men. During my early romantic relationships, I had my heart broken repeatedly as Muslim men got close and then dropped me when they realised that they couldn't make me change my views on Islam. I have stopped forming romantic relationships with Muslims, however I am unsure what will happen when I finally want to settle down and how I will explain to my parents that I cannot marry a Muslim. I kept myself in relationships with those Muslim men, even when I knew they weren't right for me, no matter how soul destroying and abusive they were, in the hope that I could marry a Muslim man who my parents would accept. I felt conflicted because I saw sex outside of marriage as both wrong and perfectly normal. My best friend and I would discuss how strange it was to be expected to have sex with only one person for the rest of your life. What if the person you married was not sexually compatible with you? I could not get married when I began to have sexual feelings, and masturbation was also taught to be sinful. In today's modern world, we must move on from the idea that you should be married to have sex, otherwise people will continue rushing into marriages because they see no alternative way to have relationships or will transgress, as I did, and find themselves riddled with guilt.

I think the depth of my internalised hatred for being a woman, a sexual object, became apparent to me during my second year at university. I went out to a club with my friends after our end of year exam. The night was supposed to be about spending the night dancing and laughing with my friends. I wore a black off the shoulder crop top, and a black skirt with an oversized shirt which was left open so that my stomach was visible. I specifically wore thick black tights, as a way to (in my mind) prevent any male interactions. I just wanted to have a good night with close friends. It was such a fun night at the beginning as I was drinking with people whom I trusted, and I had known for years and was celebrating the end of a stressful year. I felt beautiful and safe.

Later I blamed myself for what happened that night, that it was my fault that I took a sip of a drink that was brought by a stranger and which he had laced with a drug. As though through a haze of smoke, I remember being dragged out by someone I didn't know and taken to accommodation I didn't recognise. Something happened, and I was unconscious for most of it before waking up disorientated as I dressed, and this strange man let me leave. When I reported it a few days later, the bouncers at the club where I had been said that they didn't realise what had happened, they thought I was just drunk.

I still have not recovered from this experience, and I blamed myself for the longest time. I should have been more covered up; I should not have shown my belly; I should not have drunk alcohol and I should have stayed home. I had to remind myself that this was not the first time that I had been taken advantage of. As a teenager, still Muslim and fully covered from head to toe, I was still not safe from the hands of men who would pinch me or the leers that I would get from strangers in the streets. As a young woman, I was segregated from male distant relatives and non-family members within my community because if something happened, it was always the fault of the woman.

Over the years, I had heard of how sexual abuse was covered up to protect the honour of the males in my extended family and how women were stopped from reporting what happened to them. My parents understood this and took the measures they thought was appropriate to protect me from harm. When I was twelve, a distant relative who was a few years older would stare at my body and it made me feel extremely nervous. He was staying with my family at the time. I was showering one day and he managed to push the door of the bathroom open and acted as though he didn't know that I was in there. He stared at my naked body before he finally left, leaving me feeling mortified and ashamed. Nothing was said of this for years and I felt too ashamed to talk to anyone about it. Sexual violence and abuse happens in every society, however the misogynistic Islamic culture that I was raised in helped nurture a toxic environment that made me feel unsafe. At twelve and then at twenty-one years of age when I was harassed and assaulted, I believed that it was my fault for simply being a woman. Now, I recognise that sexual abuse is not warranted by how much skin is showing and is not a sexual act, it is violence and there is little the victim can do to prevent it or foresee it.

I have largely kept my beliefs about religion private. My parents still do not know even though they suspect it. I guess you could say that I am still in 'the closet' as I deny accusations that I have left Islam whenever it is raised at home. I am private about it for a few reasons. I am now mostly free to live the life I want, especially now that I am an adult. Although it was not healthy for me, I truly believe that my parents' constant surveillance on me came from a place of fear about what would happen to me if a man took advantage of me.

It's difficult to openly say that you no longer believe in Islam as Muslims tend to dismiss it as some kind of phase or delusion. Most of my ex-lovers who also happened to be Muslim told me that I am completely delusional and they either hinted or outright told me that I was not 'marriage material' because of it. I found it frustrating to debate with them because most of them followed what I see as a washed down, meek version of Islam which does not tally with what I had been taught. British Muslims from my experience may go to Friday prayer, give to charity, fast for one month a year, celebrate Eid, avoid pork, sex, and music, yet many opt to sin and then repent. I have been told that I don't follow Islam because I don't want to follow the rules. Living a double life, where you are faithful at home and sinful outside, is a common part of what it means to be Muslim in Britain today. I did not need to stop believing in Islam to be sinful.

I suppose the main difference between myself and liberal Muslims who sin and then repent, is that I don't feel guilt or the need to say sorry to anyone. Many Muslims can find peace with the knowledge that one day they will stop sinning or that God is merciful. I have come across Muslims who would lecture me about eating pork while admitting that they consume alcohol, obviously unaware that the prohibition of pork and intoxicating drinks appear side by side in the same verse of the Quran. We would go around and around in circles while debating and I always wanted to just get to the point and scream that women are not property or sexual objects, we do not deserve less inheritance and should not be made dependent on men – we are as capable as men. Whenever I tried to speak about the status of women in Islam, I was told that I clearly have not understood Islam properly, I was told to remember how well Muhammad treated his wives and that women are given a higher status in Islam. No, mothers are given higher statuses – three times that of a father – not women. I accept Islam may have been revolutionary at the time for which it developed; however, now it feels outdated in a world where women are still fighting for basic rights such as the criminalisation of marital rape in countries where Islamic law is applied. The standards are higher than they were 1400 years ago, when baby girls were buried in the desert sands. Quranic verses such as the one that instructs men to have sexual relationships with their wives whenever they want are still used today. A woman cannot initiate a divorce without going to an Islamic judge; however a man can divorce his wife by saying a simple 'divorce' three times to her. One of my teachers told me that women are emotional and if they could divorce in the same way that men can, nobody would be married.

In the end they tend to fall back on the concept that life is a test from Allah and we should have faith and do our best to die as Muslims so that we can enter paradise. The notion that your needs on earth are second best to what happens after death was unpalatable to me, it was barely living. It still makes my stomach turn to think that people believe in a God that is all loving, all merciful, who sits and watches human suffering unfold to test Muslims in a competition of who can believe the best, despite having a lack of evidence. Telling Muslims about my beliefs is difficult because it always leads to an uncomfortable debate. Sometimes, I don't want to explain to complete strangers the years of doubts, the narrations of Muhammad that didn't sit right with me, or the way that the religious sexism that I experienced suffocated me. I wish that I could just tell Muslims that I don't believe in Islam without them asking me why, because they often don't want to hear my answer and see it as some kind of rejection of them. They take it so personally, as though my lack of belief and very existence as an ex-Muslim is an insult. I have found that it is easier to lie to my family because I don't feel ready to face the consequences. I did not place a label on myself for a very long time before I came across the term 'ex-Muslim' during my late twenties. It's still not a term that I use often, but it helped me to find others who, like me, had questioned and left Islam. When I researched the term, I found that there was much abuse and so much misunderstanding about why people leave the faith. This did nothing to make me feel that I could be open about my beliefs to everyone. However, it did help me to come to terms with the fact it was okay that I did not believe in Islam and that I was not the only one who did not agree with its rules or believe that it is a perfect religion.

I find it quite interesting how people from non-Muslim backgrounds react when I have told them that I do not believe in Islam any more. It tends to come up as I often find myself explaining why I am drinking even though I have a Muslim name. I have had so many non-Muslims try to explain to me that Islam is peaceful when I tell them what made me leave the religion I was raised in and one that I had studied for many years. Muslims are indeed mostly peaceful; however Islam has a long history of violence and conquest which it cannot escape. Islamic scriptures are treated as instructions on how to live your life in accordance with a largely Arab tradition, which has been interpreted many times by scholars and ordinary Muslims all over the world. Apart from a few fringe Islamic sects, apostasy is a capital sin which can lead to severe punishment if sharia law is being applied. We are shunned and vulnerable to physical violence and the loss of those we hold dear.

I have chosen to keep my apostasy hidden from public view because it is easier this way. I have seen what happens to people who are open about why they have stopped believing in Islam, and I have decided to avoid that fate. I am one of the countless and nameless ex-Muslims who may never feel that they can express how they feel without being dismissed as stupid or insane. Many of us stay in the shadows because we are scared to hurt the people in our lives who love us and believe that we will be tormented in hell forever. I may be writing this using a pseudonym, but this is my contribution to a global movement that is not setting out to destroy religion, but instead it is demanding for us to have the freedoms which will allow us to speak and be, without the fear of losing everything that makes life worth living.

LOSING MY RELIGION

AISHA HUSSAIN

Introduction

This is not a chapter about my personal story or 'journey'; it's only a small part of a journey I'm still on and which has been a bit of a rollercoaster ride, simply trying to answer the basic questions in life: Who am I? What do I believe? And how do I best live my life? I always thought I was lucky to have grown up between several slightly different worlds and to have consistently had, as a constant in my life, elements that made it easier for me than it is for many Muslims to push boundaries and have the intellectual freedom to challenge how I was taught to see the world. In writing this, there is a risk of making it seem like I know exactly why my beliefs, my relationship to my faith and my religious identity has evolved the way it has. I may unintentionally paint an image of myself as being a much more thoughtful person than I actually am or make it seem as though before every decision in my life there was a long reflective process. But I wouldn't be entirely honest if I claimed that I can identify a clear causal relationship between particular events and the person I am today. So, while in many ways in this chapter I will be doing just that, attempting to rationalise the story of my own life by drawing a link between a series of potentially disconnected events, it should come with a huge caveat that this is simply my best effort to go back in time, reflect and give my perspective on one chapter of my life.

Islamic school years

Growing up, my family jumped around quite a bit. I was born in the UK, left for the Gulf when I was still a toddler and eventually moved to Egypt where the rest of my family lived and I spent my more formative years. I was moving to a new school at the beginning of every academic year, and, as most of these schools were international schools that didn't provide proper Islamic education, it was compensated for by my parents sending me to evening Quran classes and Islamic summer schools. These were not horrific places with angry teachers where we got canned for misreading the Quran; they had teachers who I considered as older sisters, and where I got to meet and know people who are still friends in my life today. I still have a copy of the notebook from the weekly Quran recitations in Abu Dhabi I had when I was six, with stickers and encouraging notes from my teacher on every page. And I can remember surprisingly vividly some of the plays we acted out about the stories of the prophets in Summer school in Cairo.

I now realise that this isn't quite the same experience that others, even those who were also Egyptian Muslims and international school-goers, had. For many, Islam was simply a label in the background that could be evoked or ignored depending on convenience; they never went to Quran classes or learned about the history of Islam and the stories of the prophets. For others, it was an inconvenience, a chore, something they were forced to incorporate into their lives by nagging adults. But for the earlier years in my life, Islam was neither of these things; it was the extracurricular activities, the bedtime stories and the family bonding activity. Ramadan iftars were an occasion to look forward to, praying was the time when my sister and I got to put on our over-sized praying dresses and pretend to be grown-ups. Islam was a source of positivity and a part of my life that for a long time I simply accepted.

Then, when I was around 12, my mum, brother, sister and I joined my dad, who had by then moved to London, in the UK. It was this year when I started to develop a much more thought-out outlook towards religion. I don't know if it was the change in setting and moving to the UK, the fact that I ended up attending an Islamic school, or simply that I was getting to an age when I became much more interested in defining who I was, but for the first time Islam was starting to play a very defining role in my life. I became interested in understanding why I grew up learning to pray, what the significance of the prophet stories I was taught was, and most importantly why I called myself a Muslim. Unlike my siblings who attended a normal state school in London, I went to a private Islamic girls' school. I imagine part of the incentive for my parents was that being the eldest, and at secondary school age, made it even more important to make sure I was in an Islamic environment. Years 8 and 9 of school were after all when many kids try drinking for the first time, start having boyfriends and girlfriends, and it's when many of the risks of living in a non-Muslim environment can start to manifest themselves.

It wasn't a particularly luxurious school; the facilities (or lack thereof) were hardly worth the £3k we – or our parents rather – paid, and my guess is that it wasn't very financially rewarding for the staff to be there either. So, in one way or another, most of those who were there believed in what the school stood for, either teachers who were sincere in their intention to instil Islamic values in generations to come or parents who wanted to shelter their children from society's negative influence and were willing to pay quite a bit of money to do that.

I remember everyone there being kind and genuine, but this alone was not enough to make for a good school environment and there are many things, which now, thinking back, made it far from that. Our school uniform, a long navy abaya, meant we stood out from the moment we stepped out of our homes. We were expected to wear our abayas at all times, even though most of our time was spent inside the female-only space of our school building. On the few occasions when we went out for trips or an afternoon in a nearby park – to make up for the lack of outdoor space in our school – I was constantly aware of just how odd we must have looked as a group of 20 girls all dressed in oversized navy dresses head to toe. For 11 – 13-year-old girls, it's not the best feeling to experience the eyes of strangers staring at you for looking different.

Every day during lunch hour, we held a group prayer for dhuhr[1] and there was very little room for choosing whether to join or not. A huge emphasis was placed on Arabic and Islamic studies with several hours each week dedicated to learning the Quran and tajweed.[2] None of that really bothered me; as an Arabic-speaker and someone who grew up being exposed to many Islamic classes, I already knew a lot of what we were being taught so I enjoyed being the top of my class and quickly became a teacher's pet. When it was time to pray, I was always a bit too keen – usually one of the first to lay out the prayer mats and volunteer to lead the prayers. The school uniform also slowly grew on me and as the year went on, what I wore outside of school slowly started resembling it more and more. Until, with absolutely no coercion and even slight disparagement from my parents, I went from comfortably wearing a swimsuit on weekends to donning a hijab full-time.

While I fully embraced the Islamic environment, I now think of what it must have been like for those who might have had their own doubts about Islam back then, or those at school who simply didn't feel like spending half of each lunch break praying, or covering up from head to toe just to go to class. I know for

[1] Noon prayer.

[2] Rules on the recitation of the Quran.

a fact that many girls took off the scarf the moment they got to the street corner and would, time after time, try to get out of having to pray by saying they were on their periods – an excuse that was so overused that by the middle of the year the school had a notebook for keeping track of when each girl was due. It was a space designed to teach us to obey rather than be critical, somewhere where it was okay to meddle into every private and personal detail including our monthly cycles and when we chose to kneel to God in prayer. It was an environment created to segregate us from the rest of society and suppress any early sign of rebellion and it was exactly the sort of atmosphere that set up some girls for a lifetime of leading double-lives and pretending to be people they were not. Maybe it was due to only spending one year there, or that it was before any signs of my rebellion came to surface, but I'm probably lucky it didn't have this effect on me, and by the of the year it was time to go back to Egypt.

An online world

Parallel to school and the environment I found myself in, there was a whole other world in which I was starting to immerse myself. It was a world where you could say anything you wanted and ask any question that came to your mind without having to worry about being judged – at least not by anyone whose opinion you cared about. Sure, people could accuse you of being ignorant, not being qualified or being just a kid with an internet connection, but they had absolutely no way of verifying that and you could always throw the exact same set of accusations right back at them.

I don't know how I first stumbled upon all that but it was then the beginning of the Google era when it was becoming like second-nature to run to the internet for answers on every question, and as I became more interested in religion and more observant in my day to day life I became more interested in adding an extra layer of understanding to my religiosity. In my mind, I got lucky by being born a Muslim but now I was choosing to be one. So just like a new convert teaching herself the religion from scratch; I started to Google my way to becoming a better Muslim.

Until that time, I had never had my beliefs challenged, I never had to justify that I was a Muslim or give any explanations for what I believed. Sure, I had met many non-Muslims, but it's not like non-Muslims – at least the ones I knew, thankfully – walk around asking Muslims to prove their faith. So, when in my time online I started stumbling upon online discussions and confrontations with people outright saying they disagreed with some of the things I was taught as facts, it was as surprising as it was exciting. It was an opportunity to debate openly, ask questions, and a chance for me to assert what I believed in.

I started asking many questions and working on learning the model answer to all of them. *What are the strongest scientific miracles in the Quran? What does Islam say about homosexuality? Can I pluck my eyebrows? What's the origin of the 72 virgins in heaven? What are the harms of eating pork according to science? Why does the Quran allow Muslim men to have four wives?*

Perhaps a part of me was not convinced of certain parts of religion, but mostly I wasn't looking to be convinced, I was looking for the terminology and the language and the knowledge to communicate what I was, or thought I was, already comfortable with. Then, partly because my parents were Arabs who didn't necessarily enjoy delving into sensitive subjects, I found myself looking for my own answers on more R-rated questions.

Why can't Muslim women have sex on their periods?
Would a celibate gay relationship still be a sin?
What is a paedophile?

I became an active part of that online conversation on Islam and before I knew it I was looking for answers to questions which weren't even my own. I became a 'top-contributor' on the Yahoo Answers' 'Religion and Spirituality' section and was spending most of my evenings answering questions, voting for my own answers as best answers and perfecting that online expert persona. I answered questions using words I didn't even understand. Made grand statements like 'Islam is a complete way of life. It tells man about the purpose of his creation and existence and his ultimate destiny'; 'the Quran stipulates that a man is responsible for the maintenance of his wife or wives'; 'there are some situations in which it is advantageous to society to have men marry multiple wives'; and 'Having homosexual feelings might actually be someone's way to heaven and to pleasing God which is by controlling and suppressing such desires.' But I was humble and always made sure to end my answers with 'And Allah knows best'.

The questions kept coming. *My husband wants to have anal sex, is it halal? What should I do?; What is your opinion on the Islamic dress code?; How do you define God?; Do Muslims believe in Jesus?; Can Allah and God both exist at the same time – or does the one disprove the other?.* The 12-year-old me had all the answers and they were always a search button away. Islamonline.com, Islam Q&A, Jannah.org, Harun Yahya, islamway.com, Zakir Naik Q&A, Ahmed Deedat archives … there were hundreds of online websites you could go to. I researched, read Fatwah websites and wrote up, often highly plagiarised, answers to every sort of question. I don't think I always knew how to distinguish between Sunni and Shi'a websites or between what you'd call 'mainstream' Islam and what were more on the salafi end of the spectrum. But I mastered the skill of knowing how to seem like I knew what I was talking about. I advised people who were probably at least three times my age, explained how men and women were equal in the eye of God but were created differently which is why Islam differentiates sometimes between the requirements for men and those for women. When I came across suggestions online of Muhammad being a paedophile I responded with essays on how disgraceful it was to even suggest such a thing.

But what I loved the most were questions which gave me an opportunity to illustrate that Islam was rational, scientific and compatible with reason. When the questions didn't suit my taste, I started asking questions myself which opened the door for me to come in with a different account and give the model answers I had been learning. I mastered the art of designing click-bait questions. *How can a 53-year-old man marry a 9–year-girl? Is Islam really intolerant to other faiths? Did you know that Jihad does not mean holy war? Did you know that Islam is the only non-Christian faith which makes it an article of faith to believe in Jesus? Did you ever wonder why Muslim women wear hijab? Why is Islam the fastest growing religion in the world? Is the Bible Really the Source of the Quran? Why does the Quran allow Muslim men to have four wives?*

I could go on for pages about the questions I asked, the conversations I had, and the private messages I exchanged. I made a few pen pals with people who had messaged to compliment me for spreading the message of Islam and non-Muslims who were interested in having an inter-faith dialogue. I loved not being judged for being too young but beyond everything I loved feeling like I had the answers and the means to show to myself and the world that my faith was not simply something I inherited, it was something I understood and was able to defend. I calmed down a bit eventually and started to diversify the sort of questions I was answering online – sometimes it was general questions, historical and cultural questions or dietary advice or maths homework help – but the online world never lost its importance for me. It remained a space where you could always have frank unfiltered discussions on religion, somewhere that no matter what 'it' was that you believed in, you would be able to find people willing to spend hours endorsing or challenging 'it'.

Back to school in Egypt

There were many facts, stories and parts of Islam which I loved to talk about, whether online or with friends, and there were others which even in my most devout and accepting day, I preferred to not even allow my mind think of. Almost everything related to the day of judgement fell under that second group of things, be it the signs of the day of judgement, the journey of the soul to the afterlife, the stories about what it's like to be in the grave – that time between your death and the day of judgement – or the big day itself with people running around 'naked, barefooted and uncircumcised.' For reasons I will never understand, these topics were a particular favourite for some of my school teachers back in Egypt. Unlike my UK school, it was not an 'Islamic school' per se, there was no gender segregation and definitely no abaya uniforms. Most girls in my class didn't wear hijab and I had to wear long sleeved tops under the half-sleeve school uniform top to make it work with the hijab I chose to wear. But even though formal religious education took much less of our time, Islamic stories were still casually dribbled on us just as frequently.

Sometimes out of nowhere a history and geography class would turn into a discussion about the signs of the day of judgement and the torture of the grave.

Before the day of judgement, a tribe of people called Yagoug and Magoud locked behind two mountains for thousands of years will finally be let loose. They will roam the earth looting and destroying until a big confrontation between Muslims and them. A man, who according to some stories had three-eyes and who has been chained for centuries, will escape his chains and visit every single person on earth. True believers will be able to see the word 'kafir' written on his forehead but others will blindly follow him and will be led astray. Then once you died, your grave will either feel spacious and as beautiful as a part of paradise or, you will be tormented, squeezed and perhaps even visited by a serpent. When the trumpet for the day of judgement is blown into and everyone who was ever alive comes back to life, the sun will be so close some people might drown in their own sweat.

As young teenagers, stories like this would make us sit around half in awe and half in horror. This particular side of Islam was never a big part of my personal understanding religion and their 'authenticity' like many stories from the hadith is always up for debate but let's just say they were part of the bigger picture of Islam which didn't really sit well with me. I much preferred the Islam that discussed issues of social justice and reform, the Islam which promised a better world and spoke of love and charity. In those final years of school in Egypt, I managed to incorporate this gentler side of Islam into my life. On Tuesdays I went to Islamic classes with friends where we discussed the importance of truly loving Allah, shared stories from the life of the prophet and learned how to incorporate simple Islamic values of kindness in our lives. In Ramadan, we'd go to remote areas and walk in the sun while fasting to distribute food and supplies on poor villagers. We spoke often about how unfortunate it was that the Islam we saw portrayed was so different from the Islam we knew and loved.

I also managed to weave this understanding of Islam into the parts I was less comfortable with, including the horror of the day of judgement. Islam as I knew it promised justice and as someone who was interested in the politics of the Middle East and current affairs, I knew just how unfair and unjust the world around me was. So, while the thought of the day of judgement was overwhelming and scary and I remember being kept up at night by the mere thought of it, I told myself it was ultimately part of God's justice. The promise of an afterlife meant that all the unfairness in the world will eventually balance out. If justice could be thought of as a quantifiable variable, then only God can make sure we all get our fair share when we come back to life. A favourite subject for many of those around me were stories about prophet Muhammad and the importance of loving Muhammad as if we truly knew him. And although everyone loved to emphasise that he was simply a human being not to be idolised, the intense passion by which people spoke of him and murmured prayers after each time his name was mentioned, told a different story. I could never quite get myself to that level of love and passion but to me that was more a sign that something was wrong with my faith than something wrong with Islam[3]

I also never liked Sura Al-Nisa in the Quran – which literally translates to 'the chapter of women' – but what seemed unfair to me such as inequality in inheritance or witness must have had an explanation I simply couldn't see. After all men and women were equal in the eye of Allah but if God created us differently then God must also know how to best create rules for the best of both men and women. A single drop of alcohol or kiss before marriage being haram might seem extreme. But without such clear boundaries and guidelines it would be impossible to know where to draw the line and before you knew it you'd have societies where sixteen-year olds were having babies. I could go on giving examples but the bottom line is that despite the

---

[3] They said if you loved the prophet enough (even more than your family) he might even appear in your dreams. I guess a part of me knew that if this was true then he wouldn't be visiting me in my sleep anytime.

bits and pieces which didn't entirely make sense, Islam was very much a way of living and thinking about the world that worked for me. And when it was time for me to leave Egypt for the UK again, this time for university, Islam was a part of my life I was very much planning on taking with me.

From School to University

As I was getting used to the idea of living away from my family for the first time, doing my own grocery shopping and starting to cycle everywhere, I was also getting used to the demanding social requirements of being a university 'fresher'. Being a first-year university student in the UK meant you were expected to party hard, drink and go 'crawling' from bar to bar. At the time, I had never been inside a pub in my life and when I finally got to go inside of one, disappointed doesn't even begin to explain what went through my mind. To me it was a smelly, dark and intimidating space and I couldn't relate less to the excitement or understand for the life of me what the buzz was about. I was only 17 at the time, too young to be pub crawling with anyone anyway, and almost relieved that I could use this as an excuse. It suffices to say that I didn't exactly snap into the university fresher social scene.

I was living with a Masters student and a Muslim girl I had gotten to know online through the Islamic society when I was looking for some last-minute accommodation. Before even meeting her, I had made a point of asking over email whether she wore a hijab and woke up for Fajr[4]. I later realised she wasn't nearly as keen a Muslim as I was and I must've come across as the halal-police about to ruin her experience of getting away from her Muslim parents for the first time. But in my defence, I was

[4] One of the obligatory prayers, prayed early before dawn.

simply trying to make sure I created an Islamic safe haven for myself in the middle in the non-Muslim society I was in.

When I didn't find this in the house where I was living, I went to look elsewhere and I quickly started to meet people in the mosque, prayer room and other places who looked and thought like me. It was something I was surprisingly good at doing. Just cycling to university in my very first week, when I saw a woman in a hijab and after we exchanged the smile of recognition common between hijabis, I stopped and said hi. We chatted for a bit, first in English then in Arabic when I realised she was Sudanese. In the weeks that followed she invited me over many times for a hot home-cooked meal that tasted just like home, then dropped me off back at my doorstep so I didn't have to cycle in the cold. Their family home became like a second home.

It was the same with many of the other Muslim students and families I got to meet in my first few weeks. There was a strong sense of community and I was embraced as a daughter or a younger sister by most of those I met – some gave me jars of soup and molokheya, some invited me to their living rooms, some offered their help and support. There was a feeling of familiarity and peace that I felt just by being amongst other Muslims. The prayer room on campus – a seminar room requested by the Islamic society with a few prayer mats, Qurans and Islamic books – was a place where I felt at peace and was where I went on to meet many of my closest university friends. Every now and then I tried to get involved with other non-Islamic activities on campus but maybe I never tried hard enough or maybe none of it was quite designed for someone like me. One of the few 'halal compliant' activities I managed to find in the first few weeks of university was a caving trip (a little like hiking in caves but with an added wetness factor). I signed up and on the day of the trip met up with the group and joined one of the cars driving to the location. When we arrived, we were given our wetsuits and our group leader jokingly pointed in the middle of the road and said: 'the changing rooms are here, here and here.' Everyone stripped down and started changing in the middle of the road. I stood there, confused, trying not to stare at everyone casually walking around in their underwear.

There was no way my hijab-wearing self was going to do the same so I wore the wetsuit on top of my jeans – in hindsight not the smartest thing I could've done. I don't know if anyone realised what I had done but once the wetsuit and the jeans I had underneath got wet, it was a bit like trying to move around in a sumo suit. The day wasn't too bad in the end but it was always little things like that which caused the 'I'm just not like them' LED light in my head to go on. On the way back after everyone else changed I was still there in my wet jeans and headscarf feeling a tiny bit sorry for myself. When we stopped in a pub on the way back, I went to the toilet, made wudu then prayer in a small area between the toilet and the cleaning room. I wasn't sure if my prayer would be accepted, scholarly opinions about praying in the back of pubs was not something I had looked into but it immediately made me feel a lot better.

There are many other small incidents and stories from my first year and examples of occasions when I fell back to religion for comfort. In the first term of university, a classmate of mine in Egypt passed away after a bad car accident and I found solace and comfort in simply going to the prayer room on my own and spending hours on end reading the Quran, praying and doing my own thing on my laptop. I read the Quran in lectures on my phone and started setting personal goals for memorising some of the longer Quran chapters I had forgotten. It didn't take long before I joined the Islamic Society and started getting involved in organising events and gatherings. We put together talks, dinners, and casual socials. Some were very Islamic in nature, centred around learning more about Islam and the Quran but most were simply events to socialise and provide a space for others to hang out in a place where they felt they belonged.

It was also then that an area of interest from my times on Yahoo Answers started to come to surface again. One important angle to much of what we did in the Islamic Society was 'Dawah,' the idea that we should call others, normally meaning non-Muslims, to Islam, inform them about it and do our duty in making the word of God known. Even for Muslims living in Muslim-majority countries the concept was not foreign to me but once I was living in a non-Muslim setting, it started to drive much more actively what a lot of what I did. It felt like it was my duty to not just practise my religion and practise it as much as I could, but to defend it and represent it. It was as though Islam was a child being bullied and we needed to stand up for it. I'm not sure when this idea started or when it became so popular but it was pretty standard even within Islamic circles in Egypt to talk about the importance of clearing misconceptions about Islam and to cite examples of success, with many stories of people converting to Islam. In the Islamic Society we held an 'Ask me about Islam stall' and did our best to fulfil our duty of dispelling the myths and misconceptions about Islam.

In saying all of this I don't want to fall into exaggerations about my level of religiosity, or give the impression that I did nothing but pray, read Quran and call people to Islam. Many of my friends and the people I got on with the most weren't Muslim and I still spent a fair amount of time doing more 'normal teenage things', watching American TV series and movies or listening to music. But what I can say is that I dedicated a lot of my time and effort to religion and that I chose it over what would be conventionally chosen by many people my age and in my situation of living away from home for the first time. My faith levels fluctuated, but I know that I would tear up often while prostrating in prayer. I gave the Islamic Society and helping the Muslim community a lot of my time, and to make this amount of effort there must be a level of commitment and dedication. Unlike many other forms of commitment, in the religious context the feeling of accountability feels different and is not directed towards anyone in particular. Some people who have never been religious can find it difficult to understand that the driving force for this can come from within. They insist that it can only be due to fear from religious authority or other external factor but faith, and I know this first hand, can in itself be the most powerful of drivers

Change: 'what happened?'

Sometime between this period of dedication and when I graduated, something had changed. I don't know if there was a seed of doubt all along, but if there was, I wasn't consciously trying to bury it. Of course, there were times of uncertainty but I find it difficult to believe that anyone who's ever been religious has never experienced some feeling of uncertainty. In devout circles, I've often heard people speak of fluctuating levels of Iman, of faith being like a sine curve that you just have to make sure doesn't go below a certain level, and this sine curve analogy definitely applies to what my faith was like. Sometimes being a good Muslim felt easy and other times it took a considerable amount of effort to wake up for fajr,[5] pray all my prayers and be the kind of Muslim I wanted to be. But even when my faith was at its lowest, I never would have imagined during my first year of university that four years later I wouldn't be praying at all and not even feeling guilty about it.

I don't like to dwell on what exactly changed and at what point in time. I am much more interested in the fact that transitions happen and that the person I am today is very different from the

[5] Morning prayers.

person who got excited every time I saw a hijab in the streets or the person who walked around campus postering for each upcoming ISOC event. But this doesn't mean the question of 'What happened?' is a question not worth trying to answer. The starting point must have been years before I ever realised I was doubting. Thinking and researching about religion always seemed to me like the normal and natural thing to do. It is such a big part of life, one that determines how we deal with many of the most important questions we are faced with: Why are we here? Why is there suffering in the world? What is the meaning of life?

I was never someone who could ignore these questions and religion was at the very heart of answering them. The way I thought about it, believing or not believing can make the difference between looking at life as all we have – with death being the end of it all – or as a single drop in the infinite sea of existence – with death being only the beginning. It mattered to me that I knew which side I took. Did I believe Islam was the one true religion? Did I believe in Allah? Did I believe in the Quran as the word of God? Did I believe in a day on which we would all come back to life after death and be judged for how we lived our lives? For a long time, the answers to all these questions was a decisive yes.

There were perhaps parts of the religion as a whole that I wasn't always very comfortable with but for me the good bits still far out-weighed anything else. As a comprehensive system and way of life, Islam was like the glue that held many parts of my life together. The Muslims I knew were kind, grounded and generally knowledgeable people. Islam gave them an extra reason to help each other and dedicate their time to charity. In many ways, I had no reason to think there was anything wrong with the religion they believed in and which drove so many of their good actions. But at one point far too many 'buts' and 'ifs' about other parts of the faith started to develop. I was growing more and more socially liberal and the little things I was willing to ignore before when it came to women's rights in Islam, homosexuality, the death penalty and other issues became too big to brush under the carpet. I looked into alternative interpretations, tried to understand how some of the people I loved and respected reconciled their generally liberal values with their faith, but none of it made sense to me.

If God intended for the Quran to be understood and read through an empowering feminist lens, then why not be more clear and upfront about it? If those who arrived at violent or intolerant interpretations of religion were wrong, then why did God make his one true word so obscure and prone to being misunderstood in the first place? If there is a wisdom behind everything in Islam then what is the wisdom behind the stories of Allah's wrath and anger? What was the wisdom in turning a city upside down for its people practising 'sodomy'?[6] Or sending thunderous storms on a village for worshiping idols?[7] If I had no say in being created, no control over the environment I grew up in or the way my brain functioned, then how is it fair to judge me for my actions let alone send me to an eternal paradise or hell? If God guides whom he wishes to guide, how is it fair to punish those whom he misguides? And anyway, what sort of God would demand to be constantly worshiped and praised, despite not needing it?

Some questions were naïve, childish, the sort of questions you'd expect from a toddler when they first learn the word 'why', while others were based on a much closer examination of Islam and what I knew about it. But they all pointed me to one thing. Something was off. For a very short time, I was a Selective-Muslim and even with the doubts inside me, I was still practising,

[6] Story of Lut

[7] Story of Hud

praying and fasting. But this phase of my life didn't last very long, and the inconsistencies started to feel like I was trying to fit together puzzle pieces from two different puzzle sets.

A lot of things might have been possible to ignore if it weren't for the fact that Islam makes some very big claims about itself as being the answer to many of life's questions, the guide to how to live your life, an all-encompassing system, its holy book the most perfect book on earth and its final prophet the most perfect of creation. They were claims that were part of the reason why Islam appealed to me before, but they became the reason why once certain parts of Islam started to break down for me. It all very quickly came falling down, Jenga-tower-style.

Confrontation

I suppose people first started asking questions when my most visible sign of being a Muslim went away: the hijab. It was hardly the most defining moment in my internal journey. I was still very much a believer and a Muslim when I took off the hijab. I was simply a very different Muslim from the one who had put it on 8 years earlier, one who was less inclined to make being Muslim the most visible part of her identity. The explanations I gave were simple. I no longer felt like I wanted to declare my faith to the whole world every time I stepped out of the house and I didn't want people making assumptions on what I believed. The hijab had always made me feel visible, I was one of the only girls who wore a hijab in the entire department, but suddenly it was a kind of visibility I disliked. So, after some time of playing with the idea in my head, taking off the hijab in the gym and other temporary settings, the scarf went off for good.

It wasn't until the few months after I took off the hijab, that

I really started contemplating the other doubts and questions I talked about above, and I realised that my issue wasn't so much with a piece of clothing as much as it was with placing myself with the very rigidly-defined boundaries of a particular religion. I was no longer interested in dividing the world into believer and disbeliever and I was no longer sure of which category I would even fall under myself. Eventually it became more widely known, especially to those who knew me well, that it wasn't just the hijab that went away.

My friends grew concerned about me. I knew things were being said behind my back and I was constantly being asked if I was free 'to talk', and by 'talk' people often meant 'explain'. I became so sick of questions, being expected to give explanations and elaborate on what had 'triggered my doubts'. It wasn't the fact that people asked questions that I minded, as much as what the questions were getting at. They were loaded questions, designed to act as potential leads to explain to me just how wrong I was and bring me back to the truth. The question 'What happened?' always implied that what happened was sad, unfortunate, even tragic. It was a bit like a doctor trying to diagnose an illness before curing it or making sure others didn't get it too.

In the minds of those who asked me this question, part of the explanation of what happened to me – definitely a favourite for many of my more devout Muslim friends and family members – is that at one point not practicing Islam was the easy way out. The pressure from society was mounting and being different became too much hard work. Being a good Muslim is not an easy task, its takes effort and perseverance and I failed at persevering. But I know that my faith was built on much more than convenience, it was built on top of what felt like a very strong foundation so it took more than a small push from society to push me in that direction.

Embracing the past I didn't know about

There were several elements at play. A social element and questions around what role Islam plays in society; a scientific element and how religion fits in with what we scientifically know about the origin of our species and the universe; and a purely emotional element– a change of heart of some sort. I wouldn't be able to pinpoint which ones led to my loss of faith and which were questions I contemplated as an afterthought, but one area I became particularly interested in was the history and historicity of Islam. What was the story of how Islam we knew was passed down over the past 1400 years? How did we know what we know about Muhammad? How did we decide what parts of Islam are 'authentic'? Can the Quran we have today be traced back to some original version?

The story I had been taught about how Islam formed in its early years was selective and simplistic. It was a history more interested in presenting Islam's own dogmas about its origins than presenting a balanced view of what we knew and what we didn't know. It was a 'history' that hardly reflected how notoriously difficult it is to establish even some of the most basic facts about where Muhammad lived, how the Quran was codified and how Islam emerged as a seventh-century superpower, seemingly out of nowhere. To my surprise there were in fact many theories and discussions around how and when the Quran was written and how it came together as a text, or on who Muhammad was and what motivated him. I didn't accept any particular theory but realising that there were question marks was enough.

Just like the history of the Quran, the history of Islamic civilisation that I knew reflected a single reading of history. It was a story told to enforce an identity, a feeling of superiority, and a very distinct feeling in our minds as being Muslims. The victories highlighted to us in our past were always the military ones rather than intellectual ones. We learned little about the civilisations and ideas that existed before Islam in the part of the world that today makes up the Muslim world or the multitudes of ethnicities and cultures which are still contained within the Muslim world today. What I came to realise was that both Islamic and pre-Islamic histories were so much more complex, more fascinating and incredible than I thought they were. But they weren't black and white histories of goodies and baddies. Islam emerged in a part of the world where tens of civilisations were alive yet I had never come across the names of many. As I read about the Nabateans, the Sumerians, the Phoenicians, the Sabaeans and the Assyrians who all had their own myths, their own cultures, I realised that it made much more sense to place Islam in a historical context than think of it as a special creation of an omniscient God.

Just contemplating many of these ideas was blasphemous, but to me religion had moved from the divine territory to the fascinating history territory and in that place no questions were off-limits. Islam flourished for many reasons which we may never really understand, but I preferred to see it as a human phenomenon than try to attribute everything we didn't understand to divine reasons. In Islamic history, there were many poets, scientists, philosophers, polymaths, whose names I knew and who I always thought of as being simply 'Muslim figures.' Figures such as Ibn-Sina, Al-Farabi, Al-Maari, Rumi, Ibn Rushd, and many others. What I came to realise is that many of them were doubters and sceptics, who refused simple straightforward answers and whose definitions of Islam were variable and flexible. Some wrote about the love for God, others directed questions at God, some wrote about night prayers, others wrote about wine, some wrote about all of them. There was something beautiful, powerful and almost spiritual in finding the writing of people who walked this earth a thousand years ago expressing thoughts, questions and doubts like one's own.

One commonly accepted view is that if you're a Muslim who's moving away from their faith then you're by default also moving away from your heritage, your history and almost re-defining yourself in a new light completely different from everything which was imposed on you growing up. But not believing in Islam anymore was hardly a reason for me to distance myself from it or the end point for learning about it; it just triggered in me a different kind of curiosity about the past.

More confrontations

I still don't know if I did the right thing by telling my parents I didn't believe in Islam. After a couple of conversations of beating around the bush and dodging questions about praying and taking off the hijab, I decided to drop the bomb. It was just over six months after I took off the hijab and a few months after I had admitted to myself I no longer believed and decided I had no interest in keeping up appearances. I said it directly, or some would say bluntly, that I had lost my religion ... and to say it broke their hearts would be putting it lightly. Looking back, perhaps I could've said it better, especially since I was about to admit to what was in their eyes the biggest form of betrayal to all the values with which they raised me. I had decided that the best thing to do would be to be honest and avoid going down a rabbit hole of cover-up stories and lies.

But in being honest, I was maybe being selfish. My parents had always been easy going. They were open-minded and flexible enough to allow me to travel to study abroad and live on my own and put none of the restrictions on me that many of my friends had had placed on them. But this always came with the unspoken-of condition that I would not abandon the core religious values with which they raised me. When I did abandon them, it raised all sorts of doubts in their minds about whether they had raised me right, whether they did they did the right thing by giving me the freedoms they gave me, whether they taught me everything they needed to teach me. To this day, my mum makes comments about mistakes she's made in how she taught me religion. She didn't instil the 'Aqeeda'[8] well enough in me .They probably still try to trace back what went wrong and when and what they could have done differently.

I tried to explain to them that in many ways I had no control of whether I believed or not; doubting was not something I decided to do. But in explaining this to them I often felt like I was apologising and I was never quite sure what I was apologising for. After I told my parents, an era of confrontations began. I agreed to exchanging emails with my dad about Islam and having Skype calls with my mum to explain my concerns. They arranged for me to meet with Sheikhs and scholars. Time after time I was asked to sit down to have discussions with people who said they wanted to hear from me but who actually had absolutely no interest in listening to what I had to say. They were very particular kinds of 'discussions' where the power dynamics were pre-determined. Those I spoke to were there to guide me back to the straight path and I was there to declare my intention to reflect and re-think my decision.

I was often accused of being arrogant, stubborn, of only reading and exploring what suited my taste and agenda. But none of the people I spoke to showed any interest in re-evaluating their own worldview and stance. Of course, in their eyes there was a world of difference because they were right and I was misguided. Allah had made the truth evident and I was choosing to ignore it to follow my desires. I was often asked a familiar series of loaded, leading yes-no 'questions' designed to corner

[8] The fundamentals of faith.

me in the areas of discussion they had come prepared to discuss. Questions about morality and in their view, the inevitable moral disintegration that comes with losing faith.

Familiar questions about 'whether order comes out of disorder' which were seen as decisive evidence for the existence of Allah. I was caught up in discussions around homosexuality, evolution, details of Muhammad's life-story and often had the same discussions over and over again. It was like being trapped in a situation in which whatever decision I took would be held against me. If I chose not to have discussions I was closed-minded and stubborn, but when I did they were unfruitful, frustrating, intellectually-numbing experiences. In the more positive experiences, I was given a pat on the back for being a person with a wandering mind who was going through a phase and would eventually come back.

I lost many friends, less often due to confrontation than simply feeling estranged and distanced from people who were once like siblings but with whom I no longer shared very much. Many people around me suddenly either disliked me or pitied me. I wish I could explain to these people that changing ideas doesn't change who we fundamentally are, but for many people who were brought up thinking of holding on to ideologies as the strongest marker of strength, I will always be a weak person who failed at the most important test in life.

I hoped that some of the people I loved would come to 'accept' that my beliefs had changed, but eventually I realised that acceptance is an unrealistic thing to hope for. As a friend of mine once put it, 'If they accept you then this means they stopped loving you'; it would be to give up on me finding the truth and how, after all, can a mother ever come to accept that her daughter might end up in hell? My father has since told me many times that he would never give up on me and that he has faith that someday, perhaps when he's long gone, I'll find Islam again. So, while things are now pretty much back to normal, sometimes I worry that the normality is in part based on me clinging to the unrealistic hope of being accepted and my parents clinging on to the hope that eventually I'll realise I was wrong.

Conclusion

'A little doubt is better than total credulity.'
                    Abu Alaa Al-Maarri (tenth-century Syrian poet)

I didn't choose to write this down because my story is unique, or because I have something to share with the world that's never been shared before. If anything, it's the complete opposite. It's the fact that I feel like too many people have gone through similar journeys and are made to feel like they should apologise for how their views have evolved, as if they've committed a major act of treason. But change is inevitable and to have faith imposed on us as the most defining marker of our identities and the condition for belonging is bound to make those of us who lose that faith feel alienated and left out.

I don't think there was a single moment I can point to as the moment when my worldview changed. There were many defining moments, encounters, times of reflections, lines of poetry and conversations with both strangers and people I knew well that shaped my beliefs. It's also tempting for me to try to say that society and my surroundings played no role and that it was a pure intellectual journey, but the truth is that it was a combination of many things and the environment undoubtedly acted as a catalyst. My view on many things including how to define myself[9] and the place of Islam in society, whether historically or in the present, is

[9] Between Muslim, ex-Muslim, Atheist, Agnostic, culturally Muslim and no label at all.

continuing to change. A part of me hopes it never stops changing ever so slightly. So, I guess what I'm hoping for is not for society to accept a particular viewpoint or idea, but for more people to simply see that being born into a faith shouldn't come as a curse against ever questioning it and ultimately, potentially, leaving it behind.

A SUMMARY OF LIVED EXPERIENCES

Journeys away from and re-evaluations of Islam and belief

This book was written by individuals who have lost faith in Islam. It is also written by those who see an Islam not made up of practices, force, and rigidity, but of lived and variant experiences. These individuals and their stories are not easy to dismiss. Some of the authors have deeply studied and practised Islam and they cannot be pushed aside as people with an axe to grind against Islam and their experiences dismissed. Each one of the individuals in this book, started off with a belief in their faith, which changed over time. Much like life, faith and belief and the rejection of belief do change over time, and what we have sought to highlight in this book, are the voices of a small, but growing, number of people who have left Islam; they include those who see Islam through the lens of elements that may be relevant to them and those who think they have no bearing in today's world. Just like any other faith, Islam has its believers and those who reject it, though what cannot be overlooked, is that leaving Islam may well cost some their lives in some parts of the world.

This book is an attempt to start a dialogue between those who have left Islam and Muslims. We think there is very little real dialogue or sense of civility that bridges this gulf and layered onto it are the daily social media barrages that reduce complex life-changing decisions to a few hundred characters in the gladiatorial arena that is social media. For many Muslims, 'ex-Muslims' or those who have left Islam, are seen with suspicion and their comments about Islam viewed with disgust and contempt. For some former or ex-Muslims, practising Muslims are deluding themselves about what Islam really is about and the two sides have become heavily entrenched in mistrust and a barely-concealed contempt for each other. We believe that it should never have reached this point and the personal experiences and journeys in this book paint a picture of each author as an individual just trying to live out who they want to be, with no malice in their hearts.

Each author has shared personal stories of events and experiences that have made them lose faith. Certainly, none of them has sought to damage or attack Muslims and in doing so lessen their human rights. Yet, what is clear is that all the authors have stated that they have felt that their rights and their choices were limited by faith, to the point of self-mutilation in the case of one author. How can this be right is a question that should be asked and it also begs the question of how many more people there are out there who want to speak out but cannot for fear of losing their families and receiving the vilification that comes from rejecting the faith into which they were born.

However, we remain acutely sensitive that anti-Muslim hatred and prejudice is a real and, sadly, growing phenomenon today, and each author has explicitly made clear that their intention is not to malign Muslims, it is to defend the right for people to make choices, in their own case to leave Islam, without the intense fear, harassment and vilification that often goes with it. Furthermore, some of the feelings and thoughts expressed here will make for uncomfortable reading for Muslims, but if a real connection and ongoing dialogue is to begin, these views need to be read, understood and listened to. They may not be liked, but these views and experiences cannot be dismissed out of hand in the current world we live in, which is rapidly changing.

Islam promotes self-reflection through prayer and what we hope this book will do is to also trigger some self-reflection since the experiences listed here will, no doubt, have been had by others.

Picking and choosing

In Hassan Radwan's chapter, he challenges fundamentalists in Islam who have said to him, 'You can't pick and choose!' His blunt response is that 'everyone is selective and interprets verses in the way that suits them'.

Radwan is not someone who can be marginalised as though he does not understand Islam. He spent decades learning, understanding and proselytising for Islam and lived through a time of political and social upheavals where Islam became heavily politicised due to events happening globally. He talks about the turning point being the 9/11 attacks against the United States where doubt started to creep into his mind and where he felt that he needed to reflect on what Islam meant to him. He talks about a ritualised Islam that did not meet his needs for answers around key events like 9/11 and slowly he began to look at the Quran in a critical way and to try and ask questions that had remained hidden away within him. He cites specific verses that were troubling around the 'admonishment' of women and he weighed these up with verses around protecting the rights of women. They were directly opposed to each other, something that weighed on his mind.

Radwan also gives the example of the punishments that await those in Hell and the cruel tortures that would be carried out against those people who did not believe. He paints a bleak picture, partly inferring that religion uses fear to keep the faithful on side. How could a God, who created such beauty in man, be so vengeful, Radwan ponders in his chapter.

Radwan talks about turning away from Islam and he spent four years with the Council of Ex-Muslims, before realising that he did not want to be narrowly defined in this way. He found that he had fallen into the same issue of being pigeon-holed just as he was when he said he followed the rigid ritualism and belief in the complete infallibility of the Quran. In other words, he could not move from one black and white worldview, to another one.

For Radwan, his journey saw him conclude that he did believe in 'something', and that he enjoyed connecting with God through the Islamic prayers that he knew. Even though he did not regard the Quran as the direct word of God and did not believe in its infallibility, he regarded it as a 'remarkable' piece of work that inspired him, provided the chance to connect with God, giving solace and a place of comfort deep within himself.

Radwan's journey has led him to the following conclusion. He says, 'Fundamentalists tell us – "You can't pick and choose!" My answer to them is "Watch me". The truth is all Muslims pick and choose, whether they admit it or not. Everyone is selective and interprets verses in the way that suits them.'

The role of women in Islam

One of the over-riding features in the work of several of the authors is the role of women in Islam and how innate doubts they had about the role of women in Islam were met with romanticised stories about the roles, styles of covering and the positions they played in raising families. Bangash in his chapter speaks about how Islamic patriarchy controlled what women wore and he eloquently lays down the subtle forms of male control over his sister leaving the house to go out. He paints a picture of unequal rights in a household where his sister had to deal with the religious guardianship that stifled her ability to be who she wanted to be. In Bangash's chapter we see how the layers of emotional baggage, mixed in with religious baggage, weigh down on his sister, as he places her experience within Islamic religious text. The driver is the texts that place the rights of women lower than those of men in his eyes, and which provide, in his view, the environment for abuse to take place. Yet, there is also a sadness and betrayal that plays out in his work; a betrayal around the role of females in his family and a betrayal of who and what he was and the agony of repressing the sexuality that did not fit into the framework of what his family believed a Muslim male should be. It is a story of repressed sexuality, held under the water by religion, and of women holding a lower status than that of men in his family.

On a visit to a mosque, which became his 'retreat', Bangash speaks about forbidden love and of 'the irony of being segregated with the gender you are attracted to but forbidden from loving. The homophobia he traces to the biblical story of Lot and Sodom and Gomorrah and which also found its way into the Quran. He stresses the impact of the Quranic verse and the way homosexuality is deemed to be one of the gravest sins in Islam. The psychological blow for him is clear to see as he ruminates during Wudhu,[10] thinking that with each stroke of the water on his hands and on his body, he can wash away the sexual attraction that he has for other men. The pain and the mental trauma he portrays, show a young man psychologically crushing himself in the belief that if he lives out who he is, an eternity of damnation waits for him. At home, he watched the powerlessness of the women in his family and at the mosque he tried to wash away

[1] The ablution that Muslims carry out in a ritualised fashion before prayers. It is meant to purify them for prayer.

his sexuality and his identity so that he would not experience an eternity of tortures in hell – and all the while in the company of the very sex that he was attracted to.

Or take Aisha Hussain's experiences where her upbringing in an Islamic school environment made her feel that the rules placed upon the young girls was a means of control over their bodies. Taking on the role of a religious advisor, she speaks about the advice she gave other Muslims, some of which she did to protect her belief in Islam. It was as if she was holding onto her faith, by reiterating the same passages to people online. Inquisitive and wanting to learn more she delved deeper into the works of well-known people in the Islamic world, including Zakir Naik.

For many Muslims, the chapter in the Quran termed Sura Al-Nisa, is a chapter they point to showing God's love for women. A dedicated chapter demonstrates the love that God has for women has been the mantra, though for Hussain, the lack of equal inheritance, the lower status placed on the evidence of a woman and the explicit control over women's bodies and pleasure within Islam, sowed conflicting emotions and thoughts within her. The questions she raises show a mind that was torn between her emotions, rational questions, and the inability to reconcile what she had been told with how she felt. She says, 'If God intended for the Quran to be understood and read through an empowering feminist lens, then why not be more clear and upfront about it? If those who arrived at violent or intolerant interpretations of religion were wrong, then why did God make his one true word so obscure and prone to being misunderstood in the first place? If there is a wisdom behind everything in Islam then what is the wisdom behind the stories of Allah's wrath and anger? What was the wisdom in turning a city upside down for its people practicing "sodomy"? Or sending thunderous storms on a village for worshiping idols?'

Hussain's comments will be challenging for some Muslims who

read this book, though it is not meant to instigate or create hatred towards Muslims. Nor is this book meant to be used to attack Muslims as though they are all closet 'Jihadis', 'homophobes' and 'wife beaters'. This is precisely what anti-Muslim bigots promote in an environment that is increasingly becoming more complex and difficult for Muslims, particularly visible Muslim women who are the ones most targeted at street level.

It's important to say that much of what has been written by these authors is relevant for other faiths at different times in history, and still today. This is not a book highlighting Islam as *the* worst faith of all. It is about lived experiences that some Muslims have had and which led to them leaving Islam. It will make for difficult reading for many, but their voices need to be heard. As Aisha Hussein says, 'what I'm hoping for is not for society to accept a particular viewpoint or idea, but for more people to simply see that being born into a faith shouldn't come as a curse against ever questioning it and ultimately, potentially, leaving it behind'.

Marwa Shami's experiences are harrowing and traumatic and tell of a young woman, again at odds with her feelings, though trying to fit in. From putting on the hijab to please her parents, to the heavily gender-segregated experiences that she had, in her view these pressures took something away from her development and her sense of self. She speaks about how her body changed during puberty and how, even before she could fully come to terms with her bodily changes, she was loaded with the responsibility of ensuring that her womanhood was protected and that any infractions on this purity, would be her responsibility. Any transgressions against it would also have cataclysmic ramifications for her family and their honour. This hyper-sexualisation of women's bodies, Marwa believed, was driven by the Islamic beliefs of her parents and teachers. She shares how she was penalised for having a woman's body, trying to make herself invisible for fear of attracting the attention of a boy or man and then carrying the guilt of it, weighed down by shame. It is fair to say that Marwa's very existence was based on being non-existent to the other sex.

Allied to this, the schooling Marwa received framed her future within gender-specific roles, where once again questioning anything that was historically or theologically linked to Islam was shut down. She turned to self-harm when she had a boyfriend as a form of atonement for merely encouraging affection from a male; her atonement had to come in the form of self-mutilation and blood.

Marwa, as she describes it, is 'still in the closet' and is not open about the fact that she does not believe in Islam. A series of traumas, in which religion plays a part, has left her wary and isolated, and perhaps no one will know ever the true cost of the traumatic experiences in her upbringing. What is clear though, is that the damage caused to this woman, will probably reverberate through the rest of her life, as the points of religiously-inspired abuse are manifest at times, much like an old photographic plate reveals an image when it catches the light at a certain angle.

These authors do not ask for your pity, nor do they ask for your anger or your favour. They simply ask for two things. The first is that people have a space in society where they can speak about their experiences, without fear or vilification, violence, abuse and the social ostracisation that comes from leaving faith, in this case Islam. They also ask that in creating that space, Muslims should not be targeted and their work not be used to hate or vilify others of that faith. In speaking up for tolerance towards others, they maintain that the solid foundations that society should have to defend the space for all communities and people, should be protected always.

Fiyaz Mughal and Aliyah Saleem